ABRAHAM LINCOLN SPEECHES AND WRITINGS- THE GETTYSBURG ADDRESS, THE EMANCIPATION PROCLAMATION, AND OTHERS

Bonus Content- The Declaration of Independence, The Constitution of the United States, and The Bill of Rights

By: ABRAHAM LINCOLN, JAMES MADISON, THOMAS JEFFERSON

CONTENTS

THE GETTYSBURG ADDRESS

Four score and seven years ago our fathers brought forth, upon this continent, a new nation, conceived in liberty, and dedicated to the proposition that "all men are created equal"

Now we are engaged in a great civil war, testing whether that nation, or any nation so conceived, and so dedicated, can long endure. We are met on a great battle field of that war. We have come to dedicate a portion of it, as a final resting place for those who died here, that the nation might live. This we may, in all propriety do. But, in a larger sense, we cannot dedicate—we cannot consecrate—we cannot hallow, this ground—The brave men, living and dead, who struggled here, have hallowed it, far above our poor power to add or detract. The world will little note, nor long remember what we say here; while it can never forget what they did here.

It is rather for us, the living, to stand here, we here be dedicated to the great task remaining before us—that, from these honored dead we take increased devotion to that cause for which they here, gave the last full measure of devotion—that we here highly resolve these dead shall not have died in vain; that the nation, shall have a new birth of freedom, and that government of the people by the people for the people, shall not perish from the earth.

THE EMANCIPATION PROCLAMATION

The Emancipation Proclamation is the popular name given to two complementary Presidential Proclamations issued 100 days apart from each other by United States President Abraham Lincoln during the American Civil War. These are officially known as Proclamation 93 and Proclamation 95.

Proclamation 93, the preliminary Emancipation Proclamation, was issued on September 22, 1862. It declared the freedom of all slaves in any state of the Confederate States of America as did not return to Union control by January 1, 1863. Proclamation 95, the final Emancipation Proclamation was issued on January 1, 1863. This enumerated the specific states where it applied.

PROCLAMATION 93

By the President of the United States of America.

A PROCLAMATION.

I, Abraham Lincoln, President of the United States of America, and Commander-in-Chief of the Army and Navy thereof, do hereby proclaim and declare that hereafter, as heretofore, the war will be prosecuted for the object of practically restoring the constitutional relation between the United States, and each of the States, and the people thereof, in which States that relation is, or may be, suspended or disturbed.

That it is my purpose, upon the next meeting of Congress to again recommend the adoption of a practical measure tendering pecuniary aid to the free acceptance or rejection of all slave States, so called, the people whereof may not then be in rebellion against the United States and which States may then have voluntarily adopted, or thereafter may voluntarily adopt, immediate or gradual abolishment of slavery within their respective limits; and that the effort to colonize persons of African descent, with their consent, upon this continent, or elsewhere, with the previously obtained consent of the Governments existing there, will be continued.

That on the first day of January in the year of our Lord, one thousand eight hundred and sixty-three, all persons held as slaves within any State, or designated part of a State, the people whereof shall then be in rebellion against the United States shall be then, thenceforward, and forever free; and the executive government of the United States, including the military and naval authority thereof, will recognize and maintain the freedom of such persons, and will do no act or acts to repress such persons, or any of them, in any efforts they may make for their actual freedom.

That the executive will, on the first day of January aforesaid, by proclamation, designate the States, and part of States, if any, in which the people thereof respectively, shall then be in rebellion against the United States; and the fact that any State, or the people thereof shall, on that day be, in good faith represented in the Congress of the United States, by members chosen thereto, at elections wherein a majority of the qualified voters of such State shall have participated, shall, in the absence of strong countervailing testimony, be deemed conclusive evidence that such State and the people thereof, are not then in rebellion against the United States.

That attention is hereby called to an Act of Congress entitled ''An Act to make an additional Article of War'' approved March 13, 1862, and which act is in the words and figure following:

''Be it enacted by the Senate and House of Representatives of the United States of America in Congress assembled, That hereafter the following shall be promulgated as an additional article of war for the government of the army of the United States, and shall be obeyed and observed as such:

Article —. All officers or persons in the military or naval service of the United States are prohibited from employing any of the forces under their respective commands for the purpose of returning fugitives from service or labor, who may have escaped from any persons to whom such service or labor is claimed to be due, and any officer who shall be found guilty by a court-martial of violating this article shall be dismissed from the service.

Sec. 2. And be it further enacted, That this act shall take effect from and after its passage.''

Also to the ninth and tenth sections of an act entitled ''An Act to suppress Insurrection, to punish Treason and Rebellion, to seize and confiscate property of rebels, and for other purposes,'' approved July 17, 1862, and which sections are:

''Sec. 9. And be it further enacted, That all slaves of persons who shall hereafter be engaged in rebellion against the government of the United States, or who shall in any way give aid or comfort thereto, escaping from such persons and taking refuge within the lines of the army; and all slaves captured from such persons or deserted by them and coming under the control of the government of the United States; and all slaves of such persons found (or) being within any place occupied by rebel forces and afterwards occupied by the forces of the United States, shall be deemed captives of war, and shall be forever free of their servitude, and not again held as slaves.

"Sec. 10. And be it further enacted, That no slave escaping into any State, Territory, or the District of Columbia, from any other State, shall be delivered up, or in any way impeded or hindered of his liberty, except for crime, or some offence against the laws, unless the person claiming said fugitive shall first make oath that the person to whom the labor or service of such fugitive is alleged to be due is his lawful owner, and has not borne arms against the United States in the present rebellion, nor in any way given aid and comfort thereto; and no person engaged in the military or naval service of the United States shall, under any pretence whatever, assume to decide on the validity of the claim of any person to the service or labor of any other person, or surrender up any such person to the claimant, on pain of being dismissed from the service."

And I do hereby enjoin upon and order all persons engaged in the military and naval service of the United States to observe, obey, and enforce, within their respective spheres of service, the act, and sections above recited.

And the executive will in due time recommend that all citizens of the United States who shall have remained loyal thereto throughout the rebellion, shall (upon the restoration of the constitutional relation between the United States, and their respective States, and people, if that relation shall have been suspended or disturbed) be compensated for all losses by acts of the United States, including the loss of slaves.

In Witness Whereof, I have hereunto set my hand, and caused the seal of the United States to be affixed.

Done at the City of Washington this twenty-second day of September, in the year of our Lord, one thousand, eight hundred and sixty-two, and of the Independence of the United States the eighty seventh.

PROCLAMATION 95 BY ABRAHAM LINCOLN
FINAL EMANCIPATION PROCLAMATION, 1863

Whereas, on the twenty-second day of September, in the year of our Lord one thousand eight hundred and sixty-two, a proclamation was issued by the President of the United States, containing, among other things, the following, to wit:

"That on the first day of January, in the year of our Lord one thousand eight hundred and sixty-three, all persons held as slaves within any State or designated part of a State, the people whereof shall then be in rebellion against the United States, shall be then, thenceforward, and forever free; and the Executive Government of the United States, including the military and naval authority thereof, will recognize and maintain the freedom of such persons, and will do no act or acts to repress such persons, or any of them, in any efforts they may make for their actual freedom.

"That the Executive will, on the first day of January aforesaid, by proclamation, designate the States and parts of States, if any, in which the people thereof, respectively, shall then be in rebellion against the United States; and the fact that any State, or the people thereof, shall on that day be, in good faith, represented in the Congress of the United States by members chosen thereto at elections wherein a majority of the qualified voters of such State shall have participated, shall, in the absence of strong countervailing testimony, be deemed conclusive evidence that such State, and the people thereof, are not then in rebellion against the United States."

Now, Therefore, I, Abraham Lincoln, President of the United States, by virtue of the power in me vested as Commander-in-Chief, of the Army and Navy of the United States in time of actual armed rebellion against the authority and government of the United States, and as a fit and necessary war measure for suppressing said rebellion, do, on this first day of January, in the year of our Lord one thousand eight hundred and sixty-three, and in accordance with my purpose so to do publicly proclaimed for the full period of one hundred days, from the day first above mentioned, order and designate as the States and parts of States wherein the people thereof respectively, are this day in rebellion against the United States, the following, to wit:

Arkansas, Texas, Louisiana (except the parishes of St. Bernard, Plaquemines, Jefferson, St. John, St. Charles, St. James, Ascension, Assumption, Terrebone, Lafourche, St. Mary, St. Martin, and Orleans, including the city of New Orleans), Mississippi, Alabama, Florida, Georgia, South Carolina, North Carolina, and Virginia (except the forty-eight counties designated as West Virginia, and also the counties of Berkeley, Accomac, Northhampton, Elizabeth City, York, Princess Anne, and Norfolk, including the cities of Norfolk and Portsmouth), and which excepted parts, are for the present, left precisely as if this proclamation were not issued.

And by virtue of the power, and for the purpose aforesaid, I do order and declare that all persons held as slaves within said designated States, and parts of States, are, and henceforward shall be free; and that the Executive government of the United States, including the military and naval authorities thereof, will recognize and maintain the freedom of said persons.

And I hereby enjoin upon the people so declared to be free to abstain from all violence, unless in necessary self-defence; and I recommend to them that, in all cases when allowed, they labor faithfully for reasonable wages.

And I further declare and make known, that such persons of suitable condition, will be received into the armed service of the United States to garrison forts, positions, stations, and other places, and to man vessels of all sorts in said service.

And upon this act, sincerely believed to be an act of justice, warranted by the Constitution, upon military necessity, I invoke the considerate judgment of mankind, and the gracious favor of Almighty God.

In Witness Whereof, I have hereunto set my hand and caused the seal of the United States to be affixed.

Done at the City of Washington, this first day of January, in the year of our Lord one thousand eight hundred and sixty three, and of the Independence of the United States of America the eighty-seventh.

AMNESTY TO POLITICAL OR STATE PRISONERS BY ABRAHAM LINCOLN, ISSUED: 14 FEBRUARY 1862

War Department, Washington, February 14, 1862.

The breaking out of a formidable insurrection, based on a conflict of political ideas, being an event without precedent in the United States, was necessarily attended by a great confusion and perplexity of the public mind. Disloyalty, before unsuspected, suddenly became bold, and treason astonished the world by bringing at once in the field military forces superior in numbers to the standing army of the United States.

Every department of the government was paralyzed by treason. Defection appeared in the Senate, in the House of Representatives, in the cabinet, in the Federal courts; ministers and consuls returned from foreign countries to enter the insurrectionary councils, or land or naval forces; commanding and other officers of the army and in the navy betrayed the councils or deserted their posts for commands in the insurgent forces. Treason was flagrant in the revenue and in the post-office service, as well as in the Territorial governments an in the Indian reserves.

Not only governors, judges, legislators, and ministerial officers in the States, but even whole States, rushed, one after another, with apparent unanimity, into rebellion. The capital was besieged, and its connection with all the States cut off.

Even in the portions of the country which were most loyal, political combinations and secret societies were formed, furthering the work of disunion; while, from motives of disloyalty or cupidity, or from excited passions or perverted sympathies, individuals were found furnishing men, money, and materials of war and supplies to the insurgents' military and naval forces. Armies, ships, fortifications, navy-yards, arsenals, military posts and garrisons, one after another were betrayed or abandoned to the insurgents.

Congress had not anticipated and so had not provided for the emergency. The municipal authorities were powerless and inactive. The judicial machinery seemed as if it had been designed not to sustain the government, but to embarrass and betray it.

Foreign intervention, openly invited and industriously instigated by the abettors of the insurrection, became imminent, and has only been prevented by the practice of strict and impartial justice, with the most perfect moderation, in our intercourse with nations.

The public mind was alarmed and apprehensive, though fortunately not distracted or disheartened. It seemed to be doubtful whether the Federal Government, which one year before had been thought a model worthy of universal acceptance, had indeed the ability to defend and maintain itself.

Some reserves, which perhaps were unavoidable, suffered by newly levied and inefficient forces, discouraged the loyal and gave new hopes to the insurgents. Voluntary enlistments seemed about to cease, and desertions commenced. Parties speculated upon the question whether conscription had not become necessary to fill up the armies of the United States.

In this emergency the President felt it his duty to employ with energy the extraordinary powers which the Constitution confides to him in cases of insurrection. He called into the field such military and naval forces, unauthorized by the existing laws, as seemed necessary. He directed measures to prevent the use of the post-office for treasonable correspondence. He subjected passengers to and from foreign countries to new passport regulations, and he instituted a blockade, suspended the writ of habeas corpus in various places, and caused persons who were represented to him as being or about to engage in disloyal or treasonable practices to be arrested by special civil as well as military agencies, and detained in military custody, when necessary, to prevent them and deter others from such practices.

Examination of such cases were instituted, and some of the persons so arrested have been discharged from time to time, under circumstances or upon conditions compatible, as was thought, with the public safety.

Meantime a favorable change of public opinion has occurred. The line between loyalty and disloyalty is plainly defined; the whole structure of the government is firm and stable; apprehensions of public danger and facilities for treasonable practices have diminished with the passions which prompted heedless persons to adopt them. The insurrection is believed to have culminated and to be declining.

The President, in view of these facts, and anxious to favor a return to the normal course of the administration, as far as regard for the public welfare will allow, directs that all political prisoners or state prisoners now held in military custody be released on their subscribing to a parole engaging them to render no aid or comfort to the enemies in hostility to the United States.

The Secretary of War will, however, at his discretion, except from the effect of this order any persons detained as spies in the service of the insurgents, or others whose release at the present moment may be deemed incompatible with the public safety.

To all persons who shall be so released, and who shall keep their parole, the President grants an amnesty for any past offenses of treason or disloyalty which they may have committed.

Extraordinary arrests will hereafter be made under the direction of the military authorities alone.

By order of the President:

Edwin M. Stanton, Secretary of War.

"I AM HUMBLE ABRAHAM LINCOLN."

Announcement of His Candidacy for the State Legislature. About March 1, 1832.

Fellow-Citizens: I presume you all know who I am. I am humble Abraham Lincoln. I have been solicited by many friends to become a candidate for the Legislature. My politics are short and sweet, like the old woman's dance. I am in favor of a national bank. I am in favor of the internal improvement system, and a high protective tariff. These are my sentiments and political principles. If elected, I shall be thankful; if not it will be all the same.

INJUSTICE THE FOUNDATION OF SLAVERY.

Protest of Representatives Stone and Lincoln in the Illinois Legislature Against Certain Pro-Slavery Resolutions of that Body. March 3, 1837.

The following protest was presented to the House, which was read and ordered to be spread on the journals, to wit: Resolutions upon the subject of domestic slavery having passed both branches of the General Assembly at its present session, the undersigned hereby protest against the passage of the same. They believe that the institution of slavery is founded on both injustice and bad policy, but that the promulgation of abolition doctrines tends rather to increase than abate its evils. They believe that the Congress of the United States has no power under the Constitution to interfere with the institution of slavery in the different States. They believe that the Congress of the United States has the power, under the Constitution, to abolish slavery in the District of Columbia, but that the power ought not to be exercised, unless at the request of the people of the District. The difference between these opinions and those contained in the said resolutions is their reason for entering this protest.

FINAL PUBLIC ADDRESS (1865)

Delivered on 11 April, 1865 at the White House.

We meet this evening, not in sorrow, but in gladness of heart. The evacuation of Petersburg and Richmond, and the surrender of the principal insurgent army, give hope of a righteous and speedy peace whose joyous expression cannot be restrained. In the midst of this, however, He from whom all blessings flow, must not be forgotten. A call for a national thanksgiving is being prepared, and will be duly promulgated. Nor must those whose harder part gives us the cause of rejoicing, be overlooked. Their honors must not be parcelled out with others. I myself was near the front, and had the high pleasure of transmitting much of the good news to you; but no part of the honor, for plan or execution, is mine. To Gen. Grant, his skilful officers, and brave men, all belongs. The gallant Navy stood ready, but was not in reach to take active part.

By these recent successes the re-inauguration of the national authority — reconstruction — which has had a large share of thought from the first, is pressed much more closely upon our attention. It is fraught with great difficulty. Unlike a case of a war between independent nations, there is no authorized organ for us to treat with. No one man has authority to give up the rebellion for any other man. We simply must begin with, and mould from, disorganized and discordant elements. Nor is it a small additional embarrassment that we, the loyal people, differ among ourselves as to the mode, manner, and means of reconstruction.

As a general rule, I abstain from reading the reports of attacks upon myself, wishing not to be provoked by that to which I cannot properly offer an answer. In spite of this precaution, however, it comes to my knowledge that I am much censured for some supposed agency in setting up, and seeking to sustain, the new State government of Louisiana. In this I have done just so much as, and no more than, the public knows. In the Annual Message of Dec. 1863 and accompanying

Proclamation, I presented a plan of re-construction (as the phrase goes) which, I promised, if adopted by any State, should be acceptable to, and sustained by, the Executive government of the nation. I distinctly stated that this was not the only plan which might possibly be acceptable; and I also distinctly protested that the Executive claimed no right to say when, or whether members should be admitted to seats in Congress from such States. This plan was, in advance, submitted to the then Cabinet, and distinctly approved by every member of it. One of them suggested that I should then, and in that connection, apply the Emancipation Proclamation to the theretofore excepted parts of Virginia and Louisiana; that I should drop the suggestion about apprenticeship for freed-people, and that I should omit the protest against my own power, in regard to the admission of members to Congress; but even he approved every part and parcel of the plan which has since been employed or touched by the action of Louisiana. The new constitution of Louisiana, declaring emancipation for the whole State, practically applies the Proclamation to the part previously excepted. It does not adopt apprenticeship for freed-people; and it is silent, as it could not well be otherwise, about the admission of members to Congress. So that, as it applies to Louisiana, every member of the Cabinet fully approved the plan. The message went to Congress, and I received many commendations of the plan, written and verbal; and not a single objection to it, from any professed emancipationist, came to my knowledge, until after the news reached Washington that the people of Louisiana had begun to move in accordance with it. From about July 1862, I had corresponded with different persons, supposed to be interested, seeking a reconstruction of a State government for Louisiana. When the message of 1863, with the plan before mentioned, reached New-Orleans, Gen. Banks wrote me that he was confident the people, with his military co-operation, would reconstruct, substantially on that plan. I wrote him, and some of them to try it; they tried it, and the result is known. Such only has been my agency in getting up the Louisiana government. As to sustaining it, my promise is out, as before stated. But, as bad promises are better broken than kept, I shall treat this as a bad promise, and break it, whenever I shall be convinced that keeping it is adverse to the public interest. But I have not yet been so convinced.

I have been shown a letter on this subject, supposed to be an able one, in which the writer expresses regret that my mind has not seemed to be definitely fixed on the question whether the seceding States, so called, are in the Union or out of it. It would perhaps, add astonishment to his regret, were he to learn that since I have found professed Union men endeavoring to make that question, I have purposely forborne any public expression upon it. As appears to me that question has not been, nor yet is, a practically material one, and that any discussion of it, while it thus remains practically immaterial, could have no effect other than the mischievous one of dividing our friends. As yet, whatever it may hereafter become, that question is bad, as the basis of a controversy, and good for nothing at all—a merely pernicious abstraction.

We all agree that the seceded States, so called, are out of their proper relation with the Union; and that the sole object of the government, civil and military, in regard to those States is to again get them into that proper practical relation. I believe it is not only possible, but in fact, easier to do this, without deciding, or even considering, whether these States have ever been out of the Union, than with it. Finding themselves safely at home, it would be utterly immaterial whether they had ever been abroad. Let us all join in doing the acts necessary to restoring the proper practical relations between these States and the Union; and each forever after, innocently indulge his own opinion whether, in doing the acts, he brought the States from without, into the Union, or only gave them proper assistance, they never having been out of it.

The amount of constituency, so to speak, on which the new Louisiana government rests, would be more satisfactory to all, if it contained fifty, thirty, or even twenty thousand, instead of only about twelve thousand, as it does. It is also unsatisfactory to some that the elective franchise is not given to the colored man. I would myself prefer that it were now conferred on the very intelligent, and on those who serve our cause as soldiers. Still the question is not whether the Louisiana government, as it stands, is quite all that is desirable. The question is, "Will it be wiser to take it as it is, and help to improve it; or to reject, and disperse it?" "Can Louisiana be brought into proper practical relation with the Union sooner by sustaining, or by discarding her new State government?"

Some twelve thousand voters in the heretofore slave-state of Louisiana have sworn allegiance to the Union, assumed to be the rightful political power of the State, held elections, organized a State government, adopted a free-state constitution, giving the benefit of public schools equally to black and white, and empowering the Legislature to confer the elective franchise upon the colored man. Their Legislature has already voted to ratify the constitutional amendment recently passed by Congress, abolishing slavery throughout the nation. These twelve thousand persons are thus fully committed to the Union, and to perpetual freedom in the state— committed to the very things, and nearly all the things the nation wants—and they ask the nations recognition and its assistance to make good their committal. Now, if we reject, and spurn them, we do our utmost to disorganize and disperse them. We in effect say to the white men "You are worthless, or worse—we will neither help you, nor be helped by you." To the blacks we say "This cup of liberty which these, your old masters, hold to your lips, we will dash from you, and leave you to the chances of gathering the spilled and scattered contents in some vague and undefined when, where, and how." If this course, discouraging and paralyzing both white and black, has any tendency to bring Louisiana into proper practical relations with the Union, I have, so far, been unable to perceive it. If, on the contrary, we recognize, and sustain the new government of Louisiana the converse of all this is made true. We encourage the hearts, and nerve the arms of the twelve thousand to adhere to their work, and argue for it, and proselyte for it, and fight for it, and feed it, and grow it, and ripen it to a complete success. The colored man too, in seeing all united for him, is inspired with vigilance, and energy, and daring, to the same end. Grant that he desires the elective franchise, will he not attain it sooner by saving the already advanced steps toward it, than by running backward over them? Concede that the new government of Louisiana is only to what it should be as the egg is to the fowl, we shall sooner have the fowl by hatching the egg than by smashing it? Again, if we reject Louisiana, we also reject one vote in favor of the proposed amendment to the national Constitution. To meet this proposition, it has been argued that no more than three fourths of those States which have not attempted secession are necessary to validly ratify the amendment. I do not commit myself against this, further than to say that such a ratification would be questionable, and sure to be persistently questioned; while a ratification by three-fourths of all the States would be unquestioned and unquestionable.

I repeat the question, "Can Louisiana be brought into proper practical relation with the Union sooner by sustaining or by discarding her new State Government?

What has been said of Louisiana will apply generally to other States. And yet so great peculiarities pertain to each state, and such important and sudden changes occur in the same state; and withal, so new and unprecedented is the whole case, that no exclusive, and inflexible plan can be safely prescribed as to details and colatterals [sic]. Such exclusive, and inflexible plan, would surely become a new entanglement. Important principles may, and must, be inflexible.

In the present "situation" as the phrase goes, it may be my duty to make some new announcement to the people of the South. I am considering, and shall not fail to act, when satisfied that action will be proper.

EXECUTIVE ORDER 2 SIGNED BY ABRAHAM LINCOLN

Rewards For The Arrest Of Felons From Foreign Countries Committing Felonies In The United States

To all whom these presents may concern: Whereas, for some time past, evil-disposed persons have crossed the borders of the United States, or entered their ports by sea from countries where they are tolerated, and have committed capital felonies against the property and life of American citizens, as well in the cities as in the rural districts of the country: Now, therefore, in the name and by the authority of the President of the United States, I do hereby make known that a reward of one thousand dollars will be paid, at this Department, for the capture of each of such offenders upon his conviction by a civil or military tribunal, to whomsoever shall arrest and deliver such offenders into the custody of the civil or military authorities of the United States. And the like reward will be paid, upon the same terms, for the capture of any such persons so entering the United States, whose offences shall be committed subsequently to the publication of this notice. A reward of five hundred dollars will be paid, upon conviction, for the arrest of any person who shall have aided and abetted offenders of the class before named within the territory of the United States. Given under my hand, and the seal of the Department of State, at Washington, this fourth day of April, A. D. 1865.

ABRAHAM LINCOLN'S FIRST INAUGURAL ADDRESS

Lincoln's First Inaugural Address was delivered on March 4, 1861, a month after seven slave states declared that they had seceded to form the Confederate States of America and a month before the Battle of Fort Sumter. In it Lincoln argues that the union of the states is perpetual and describes a policy of non-interference toward slavery in the South, including support of the Corwin Amendment. This edition is from Lincoln's Life and Works.

First Inaugural Address.

Delivered at Washington, D. C. March 4, 1861.

Fellow-citizens of the United States: In compliance with a custom as old as the government itself, I appear before you to address you briefly, and to take in your presence the oath prescribed by the Constitution of the United States to be taken by the President "before he enters on the execution of his office."

I do not consider it necessary at present for me to discuss those matters of administration about which there is no special anxiety or excitement.

Apprehension seems to exist among the people of the Southern States that by the accession of a Republican administration their property and their peace and personal security are to be endangered. There has never been any reasonable cause for such apprehension. Indeed, the most ample evidence to the contrary has all the while existed and been open to their inspection. It is found in nearly all the published speeches of him who now addresses you. I do but quote from one of those speeches when I declare that "I have no purpose, directly or indirectly, to interfere with the institution of slavery in the States where it exists. I believe I have no lawful right to do so, and I have no inclination to do so." Those who nominated and elected me did so with full knowledge that I had made this and many similar declarations, and had never recanted them. And, more than this, they placed in the platform for my acceptance, and as a law to themselves and to me, the clear and emphatic resolution which I now read:

Resolved, That the maintenance inviolate of the rights of the States, and especially the right of each State to order and control its own domestic institutions according to its own judgment exclusively, is essential to that balance of power on which the perfection and endurance of our political fabric depend, and we denounce the lawless invasion by armed force of the soil of any State or Territory, no matter under what pretext, as among the gravest of crimes.

I now reiterate these sentiments; and, in doing so, I only press upon the public attention the most conclusive evidence of which the case is susceptible, that the property, peace, and security of no section are to be in any wise endangered by the now incoming administration. I add, too, that all the protection which, consistently with the Constitution and the laws, can be given, will be cheerfully given to all the States when lawfully demanded, for whatever cause—as cheerfully to one section as to another.

There is much controversy about the delivering up of fugitives from service or labor. The clause I now read is as plainly written in the Constitution as any other of its provisions:

No person held to service or labor in one State, under the laws thereof, escaping into another, shall in consequence of any law or regulation therein be discharged from such service or labor, but shall be delivered up on claim of the party to whom such service or labor may be due.

It is scarcely questioned that this provision was intended by those who made it for the reclaiming of what we call fugitive slaves; and the intention of the lawgiver is the law. All members of Congress swear their support to the whole Constitution—to this provision as much as to any other. To the proposition, then, that slaves whose cases come within the terms of this clause "shall be delivered up," their oaths are unanimous. Now, if they would make the effort in good temper, could they not with nearly equal unanimity frame and pass a law by means of which to keep good that unanimous oath?

There is some difference of opinion whether this clause should be enforced by national or by State authority; but surely that difference is not a very material one. If the slave is to be surrendered, it can be of but little consequence to him or to others by which authority it is done. And should anyone in any case be content that his oath shall go unkept on a merely unsubstantial controversy as to how it shall be kept?

Again, in any law upon this subject, ought not all the safeguards of liberty known in civilized and humane jurisprudence to be introduced, so that a free man be not, in any case, surrendered as a slave? And might it not be well at the same time to provide by law for the enforcement of that clause in the Constitution which guarantees that "the citizen of each State shall be entitled to all privileges and immunities of citizens in the several States."

I take the official oath to-day with no mental reservations, and with no purpose to construe the Constitution or laws by any hypercritical rules. And while I do not choose now to specify particular acts of Congress as proper to be enforced, I do suggest that it will be much safer for all, both in official and private stations, to conform to and abide by all those acts which stand unrepealed, than to violate any of them, trusting to find impunity in having them held to be unconstitutional.

It is seventy-two years since the first inauguration of a President under our National Constitution. During that period fifteen different and greatly distinguished citizens have, in succession, administered the executive branch of the government. They have conducted it through many perils, and generally with great success. Yet, with all this scope of precedent, I now enter upon the same task for the brief constitutional term of four years under great and peculiar difficulty. A disruption of the Federal Union, heretofore only menaced, is now formidably attempted.

I hold that, in contemplation of universal law and of the Constitution, the Union of these States is perpetual. Perpetuity is implied, if not expressed, in the fundamental law of all national governments. It is safe to assert that no government proper ever had a provision in its organic law for its own termination. Continue to execute all the express provisions of our National Constitution, and the Union will endure forever—it being impossible to destroy it except by some action not provided for in the instrument itself.

Again, if the United States be not a government proper, but an association of States in the nature of contract merely, can it, as a contract, be peaceably unmade by less than all the parties who made it? One party to a contract may violate it—break it, so to speak; but does it not require all to lawfully rescind it?

Descending from these general principles, we find the proposition that, in legal contemplation the Union is perpetual confirmed by the history of the Union itself. The Union is much older than the Constitution. It was formed, in fact, by the Articles of Association in 1774. It was matured and continued by the Declaration of Independence in 1776. It was further matured, and the faith of all the then thirteen States expressly plighted and engaged that it should be perpetual, by the Articles of Confederation in 1778. And, finally, in 1787 one of the declared objects for ordaining and establishing the Constitution was "to form a more perfect Union."

But if the destruction of the Union by one or by a part only of the States be lawfully possible, the Union is less perfect than before the Constitution, having lost the vital element of perpetuity.

It follows from these views that no State upon its own mere motion can lawfully get out of the Union; that resolves and ordinances to that effect are legally void; and that acts of violence, within any State or States, against the authority of the United States, are insurrectionary or revolutionary, according to circumstances.

I therefore consider that, in view of the Constitution and the laws, the Union is unbroken; and to the extent of my ability I shall take care, as the Constitution itself expressly enjoins upon me, that the laws of the Union be faithfully executed in all the States. Doing this I deem to be only a simple duty on my part; and I shall perform it so far as practicable, unless my rightful masters, the American people, shall withhold the requisite means, or in some authoritative manner direct the contrary. I trust this will not be regarded as a menace, but only as the declared purpose of the Union that it will constitutionally defend and maintain itself.

In doing this there needs to be no bloodshed or violence; and there shall be none, unless it be forced upon the national authority. The power confided to me will be used to hold, occupy, and possess the property and places belonging to the government, and to collect the duties and imposts; but beyond what may be necessary for these objects, there will be no invasion, no using of force against or among the people anywhere. Where hostility to the United States, in any interior locality, shall be so great and universal as to prevent competent resident citizens from holding the Federal offices, there will be no attempt to force obnoxious strangers among the people for that object. While the strict legal right may exist in the government to enforce the exercise of these offices, the attempt to do so would be so irritating, and so nearly impracticable withal, that I deem it better to forego for the time the uses of such offices.

The mails, unless repelled, will continue to be furnished in all parts of the Union. So far as possible, the people everywhere shall have that sense of perfect security which is most favorable to calm thought and reflection. The course here indicated will be followed unless current events and experience shall show a modification or change to be proper, and in every case and exigency my best discretion will be exercised according to circumstances actually existing, and with a view and a hope of a peaceful solution of the national troubles and the restoration of fraternal sympathies and affections.

That there are persons in one section or another who seek to destroy the Union at all events, and are glad of any pretext to do it, I will neither affirm nor deny; but if there be such, I need address no word to them. To those, however, who really love the Union may I not speak?

Before entering upon so grave a matter as the destruction of our national fabric, with all its benefits, its memories, and its hopes, would it not be wise to ascertain precisely why we do it? Will you hazard so desperate a step while there is any possibility that any portion of the ills you fly from have no real existence? Will you, while the certain ills you fly to are greater than all the real ones you fly from—will you risk the commission of so fearful a mistake?

All profess to be content in the Union if all constitutional rights can be maintained. Is it true, then, that any right, plainly written in the Constitution, has been denied? I think not. Happily the human mind is so constituted that no party can reach to the audacity of doing this. Think, if you can, of a single instance in which a plainly written provision of the Constitution has ever been denied. If by the mere force of numbers a majority should deprive a minority of any clearly written constitutional right, it might, in a moral point of view, justify revolution—certainly would if such a right were a vital one. But such is not our case. All the vital rights of minorities and of individuals are so plainly assured to them by affirmations and negations, guarantees and prohibitions, in the Constitution, that controversies never arise concerning them. But no organic law can ever be framed with a provision specifically applicable to every question which may occur in practical administration. No foresight can anticipate, nor any document of reasonable length contain, express provisions for all possible questions. Shall fugitives from labor be surrendered by national or by State authority? The Constitution does not expressly say. May Congress prohibit slavery in the Territories? The Constitution does not expressly say. Must Congress protect slavery in the Territories? The Constitution does not expressly say.

From questions of this class spring all our constitutional controversies, and we divide upon them into majorities and minorities. If the minority will not acquiesce, the majority must, or the government must cease. There is no other alternative; for continuing the government is acquiescence on one side or the other.

If a minority in such case will secede rather than acquiesce, they make a precedent which in turn will divide and ruin them; for a minority of their own will secede from them whenever a majority refuses to be controlled by such minority. For instance, why may not any portion of a new confederacy a year or two hence arbitrarily secede again, precisely as portions of the present Union now claim to secede from it? All who cherish disunion sentiments are now being educated to the exact temper of doing this.

Is there such perfect identity of interests among the States to compose a new Union, as to produce harmony only, and prevent renewed secession?

Plainly, the central idea of secession is the essence of anarchy. A majority held in restraint by constitutional checks and limitations, and always changing easily with deliberate changes of popular opinions and sentiments, is the only true sovereign of a free people. Whoever rejects it does, of necessity, fly to anarchy or to despotism. Unanimity is impossible; the rule of a minority, as a permanent arrangement, is wholly inadmissible; so that, rejecting the majority principle, anarchy or despotism in some form is all that is left.

I do not forget the position, assumed by some, that constitutional questions are to be decided by the Supreme Court; nor do I deny that such decisions must be binding, in any case, upon the parties to a suit, as to the object of that suit, while they are also entitled to very high respect and consideration in all parallel cases by all other departments of the government. And while it is obviously possible that such decision may be erroneous in any given case, still the evil effect following it, being limited to that particular case, with the chance that it may be overruled and never become a precedent for other cases, can better be borne than could the evils of a different practice. At the same time, the candid citizen must confess that if the policy of the government, upon vital questions affecting the whole people, is to be irrevocably fixed by decisions of the Supreme Court, the instant they are made, in ordinary litigation between parties in personal actions, the people will have ceased to be their own rulers, having to that extent practically resigned their government into the hands of that eminent tribunal. Nor is there in this view any assault upon the court or the judges. It is a duty from which they may not shrink to decide cases properly brought before them, and it is no fault of theirs if others seek to turn their decisions to political purposes.

One section of our country believes slavery is right, and ought to be extended, while the other believes it is wrong, and ought not to be extended. This is the only substantial dispute. The fugitive-slave clause of the Constitution, and the law for the suppression of the foreign slave-trade, are each as well enforced, perhaps, as any law can ever be in a community where the moral sense of the people imperfectly supports the law itself. The great body of the people abide by the dry legal obligation in both cases, and a few break over in each. This, I think, cannot be perfectly cured; and it would be worse in both cases after the separation of the sections than before. The foreign slave-trade, now imperfectly suppressed, would be ultimately revived, without restriction, in one section, while fugitive slaves, now only partially surrendered, would not be surrendered at all by the other.

Physically speaking, we cannot separate. We cannot remove our respective sections from each other, nor build an impassable wall between them. A husband and wife may be divorced, and go out of the presence and beyond the reach of each other; but the different parts of our country cannot do this. They cannot but remain face to face, and intercourse, either amicable or hostile, must continue between them. Is it possible, then, to make that intercourse more advantageous or more satisfactory after separation than before? Can aliens make treaties easier than friends can make laws? Can treaties be more faithfully enforced between aliens than laws can among friends? Suppose you go to war, you cannot fight always; and when, after much loss on both sides, and no gain on either, you cease fighting, the identical old questions as to terms of intercourse are again upon you.

This country, with its institutions, belongs to the people who inhabit it. Whenever they shall grow weary of the existing government, they can exercise their constitutional right of amending it, or their revolutionary right to dismember or overthrow it. I cannot be ignorant of the fact that many worthy and patriotic citizens are desirous of having the National Constitution amended. While I make no recommendation of amendments, I fully recognize the rightful authority of the people over the whole subject, to be exercised in either of the modes prescribed in the instrument itself; and I should, under existing circumstances, favor rather than oppose a fair opportunity being afforded the people to act upon it. I will venture to add that to me the convention mode seems preferable, in that it allows amendments to originate with the people themselves, instead of only permitting them to take or reject propositions originated by others not especially chosen for the purpose, and which might not be precisely such as they would wish to either accept or refuse. I understand a proposed amendment to the Constitution—which amendment, however, I have not seen—has passed Congress, to the effect that the Federal Government shall never interfere with the domestic institutions of the States, including that of persons held to service. To avoid misconstruction of what I have said, I depart from my purpose not to speak of particular amendments so far as to say that, holding such a provision to now be implied constitutional law, I have no objection to its being made express and irrevocable.

The chief magistrate derives all his authority from the people, and they have conferred none upon him to fix terms for the separation of the States. The people themselves can do this also if they choose; but the executive, as such, has nothing to do with it. His duty is to administer the present government, as it came to his hands, and to transmit it, unimpaired by him, to his successor.

Why should there not be a patient confidence in the ultimate justice of the people? Is there any better or equal hope in the world? In our present differences is either party without faith of being in the right? If the Almighty Ruler of Nations, with his eternal truth and justice, be on your side of the North, or on yours of the South, that truth and that justice will surely prevail by the judgment of this great tribunal of the American people.

By the frame of the government under which we live, this same people have wisely given their public servants but little power for mischief; and have, with equal wisdom, provided for the return of that little to their own hands at very short intervals. While the people retain their virtue and vigilance, no administration, by any extreme of wickedness or folly, can very seriously injure the government in the short space of four years.

My countrymen, one and all, think calmly and well upon this whole subject. Nothing valuable can be lost by taking time. If there be an object to hurry any of you in hot haste to a step which you would never take deliberately, that object will be frustrated by taking time; but no good object can be frustrated by it. Such of you as are now dissatisfied, still have the old Constitution unimpaired, and, on the sensitive point, the laws of your own framing under it; while the new administration will have no immediate power, if it would, to change either. If it were admitted that you who are dissatisfied hold the right side in the dispute, there still is no single good reason for precipitate action. Intelligence, patriotism, Christianity, and a firm reliance on Him who has never yet forsaken this favored land, are still competent to adjust in the best way all our present difficulty.

In your hands, my dissatisfied fellow-countrymen, and not in mine, is the momentous issue of civil war. The government will not assail you. You can have no conflict without being yourselves the aggressors. You have no oath registered in heaven to destroy the government, while I shall have the most solemn one to "preserve, protect, and defend it."

I am loath to close. We are not enemies, but friends. We must not be enemies. Though passion may have strained, it must not break our bonds of affection. The mystic chords of memory, stretching from every battle-field and patriot grave to every living heart and hearthstone all over this broad land, will yet swell the chorus of the Union when again touched, as surely they will be, by the better angels of our nature.

ABRAHAM LINCOLN'S SECOND INAUGURAL ADDRESS

Second Inaugural Address.

Delivered at Washington, D. C. March 4, 1865.

Fellow-countrymen: At this second appearing to take the oath of the presidential office, there is less occasion for an extended address than there was at the first. Then a statement, somewhat in detail, of a course to be pursued, seemed fitting and proper. Now, at the expiration of four years, during which public declarations have been constantly called forth on every point and phase of the great contest which still absorbs the attention and engrosses the energies of the nation, little that is new could be presented. The progress of our arms, upon which all else chiefly depends, is as well known to the public as to myself; and it is, I trust, reasonably satisfactory and encouraging to all. With high hope for the future, no prediction in regard to it is ventured.

On the occasion corresponding to this four years ago, all thoughts were anxiously directed to an impending civil war. All dreaded it—all sought to avert it. While the inaugural address was being delivered from this place, devoted altogether to saving the Union without war, insurgent agents were in the city seeking to destroy it without war—seeking to dissolve the Union, and divide effects, by negotiation. Both parties deprecated war; but one of them would make war rather than let the nation survive; and the other would accept war rather than let it perish. And the war came.

One-eighth of the whole population were colored slaves, not distributed generally over the Union, but localized in the Southern part of it. These slaves constituted a peculiar and powerful interest. All knew that this interest was, somehow, the cause of the war. To strengthen, perpetuate, and extend this interest was the object for which the insurgents would rend the Union, even by war; while the government claimed no right to do more than to restrict the territorial enlargement of it.

Neither party expected for the war the magnitude or the duration which it has already attained. Neither anticipated that the cause of the conflict might cease with, or even before, the conflict itself should cease. Each looked for an easier triumph, and a result less fundamental and astounding. Both read the same Bible, and pray to the same God; and each invokes his aid against the other. It may seem strange that any men should dare to ask a just God's assistance in wringing their bread from the sweat of other men's faces; but let us judge not, that we be not judged. The prayers of both could not be answered—that of neither has been answered fully.

The Almighty has his own purposes. "Woe unto the world because of offenses! for it must needs be that offenses come; but woe to that man by whom the offense cometh." If we shall suppose that American slavery is one of those offenses which, in the providence of God, must needs come, but which, having continued through his appointed time, he now wills to remove, and that he gives to both North and South this terrible war, as the woe due to those by whom the offense came, shall we discern therein any departure from those divine attributes which the believers in a living God always ascribe to him? Fondly do we hope—fervently do we pray—that this mighty scourge of war may speedily pass away. Yet, if God wills that it continue until all the wealth piled by the bondman's two hundred and fifty years of unrequited toil shall be sunk, and until every drop of blood drawn with the lash shall be paid by another drawn with the sword, as was said three thousand years ago, so still it must be said, "The judgments of the Lord are true and righteous altogether."

With malice toward none; with charity for all; with firmness in the right, as God gives us to see the right, let us strive on to finish the work we are in; to bind up the nation's wounds; to care for him who shall have borne the battle, and for his widow, and his orphan—to do all which may achieve and cherish a just and lasting peace among ourselves, and with all nations.

FIRST STATE OF THE UNION ADDRESS (1861)

Fellow-Citizens of the Senate and House of Representatives:

In the midst of unprecedented political troubles we have cause of great gratitude to God for unusual good health and most abundant harvests.

You will not be surprised to learn that in the peculiar exigencies of the times our intercourse with foreign nations has been attended with profound solicitude, chiefly turning upon our own domestic affairs.

A disloyal portion of the American people have during the whole year been engaged in an attempt to divide and destroy the Union. A nation which endures factious domestic division is exposed to disrespect abroad, and one party, if not both, is sure sooner or later to invoke foreign intervention.

Nations thus tempted to interfere are not always able to resist the counsels of seeming expediency and ungenerous ambition, although measures adopted under such influences seldom fail to be unfortunate and injurious to those adopting them.

The disloyal citizens of the United States who have offered the ruin of our country in return for the aid and comfort which they have invoked abroad have received less patronage and encouragement than they probably expected. If it were just to suppose, as the insurgents have seemed to assume, that foreign nations in this case, discarding all moral, social, and treaty obligations, would act solely and selfishly for the most speedy restoration of commerce, including especially the acquisition of cotton, those nations appear as yet not to have seen their way to their object more directly or clearly through the destruction than through the preservation of the Union. If we could dare to believe that foreign nations are actuated by no higher principle than this, I am quite sure a sound argument could be made to show them that they can reach their aim more readily and easily by aiding to crush this rebellion than by giving encouragement to it.

The principal lever relied on by the insurgents for exciting foreign nations to hostility against us, as already intimated, is the embarrassment of commerce. Those nations, however, not improbably saw from the first that it was the Union which made as well our foreign as our domestic commerce. They can scarcely have failed to perceive that the effort for disunion produces the existing difficulty, and that one strong nation promises more durable peace and a more extensive, valuable, and reliable commerce than can the same nation broken into hostile fragments.

It is not my purpose to review our discussions with foreign states, because, whatever might be their wishes or dispositions, the integrity of our country and the stability of our Government mainly depend not upon them, but on the loyalty, virtue, patriotism, and intelligence of the American people. The correspondence itself, with the usual reservations, is herewith submitted.

I venture to hope it will appear that we have practiced prudence and liberality toward foreign powers, averting causes of irritation and with firmness maintaining our own rights and honor.

Since, however, it is apparent that here, as in every other state, foreign dangers necessarily attend domestic difficulties, I recommend that adequate and ample measures be adopted for maintaining the public defenses on every side. While under this general recommendation provision for defending our seacoast line readily occurs to the mind, I also in the same connection ask the attention of Congress to our great lakes and rivers. It is believed that some fortifications and depots of arms and munitions, with harbor and navigation improvements, all at well-selected points upon these, would be of great importance to the national defense and preservation. I ask attention to the views of the Secretary of War, expressed in his report, upon the same general subject.

I deem it of importance that the loyal regions of east Tennessee and western North Carolina should be connected with Kentucky and other faithful parts of the Union by railroad. I therefore recommend, as a military measure, that Congress provide for the construction of such road as speedily as possible. Kentucky no doubt will cooperate, and through her legislature make the most judicious selection of a line. The northern terminus must connect with some existing railroad, and whether the route shall be from Lexington or Nicholasville to the Cumberland Gap, or from Lebanon to the Tennessee line, in the direction of Knoxville, or on some still different line, can easily be determined. Kentucky and the General Government cooperating, the work can be completed in a very short time, and when done it will be not only of vast present usefulness, but also a valuable permanent improvement, worth its cost in all the future.

Some treaties, designed chiefly for the interests of commerce, and having no grave political importance, have been negotiated, and will be submitted to the Senate for their consideration.

Although we have failed to induce some of the commercial powers to adopt a desirable melioration of the rigor of maritime war, we have removed all obstructions from the way of this humane reform except such as are merely of temporary and accidental occurrence.

I invite your attention to the correspondence between Her Britannic Majesty's minister accredited to this Government and the Secretary of State relative to the detention of the British ship Perthshire in June last by the United States steamer Massachusetts for a supposed breach of the blockade. As this detention was occasioned by an obvious misapprehension of the facts, and as justice requires that we should commit no belligerent act not rounded in strict right as sanctioned by public law, I recommend that an appropriation be made to satisfy the reasonable demand of the owners of the vessel for her detention.

I repeat the recommendation of my predecessor in his annual message to Congress in December last in regard to the disposition of the surplus which will probably remain after satisfying the claims of American citizens against China, pursuant to the awards of the commissioners under the act of the 3d of March, 1859. If, however, it should not be deemed advisable to carry that recommendation into effect, I would suggest that authority be given for investing the principal, over the proceeds of the surplus referred to, in good securities, with a view to the satisfaction of such other just claims of our citizens against China as are not unlikely to arise hereafter in the course of our extensive trade with that Empire.

By the act of the 5th of August last Congress authorized the President to instruct the commanders of suitable vessels to defend themselves against and to capture pirates. This authority has been exercised in a single instance only. For the more effectual protection of our extensive and valuable commerce in the Eastern seas especially, it seems to me that it would also be advisable to authorize the commanders of sailing vessels to recapture any prizes which pirates may make of United States vessels and their cargoes, and the consular courts now established by law in Eastern countries to adjudicate the cases in the event that this should not be objected to by the local authorities.

If any good reason exists why we should persevere longer in withholding our recognition of the independence and sovereignty of Hayti and Liberia, I am unable to discern it. Unwilling, however, to inaugurate a novel policy in regard to them without the approbation of Congress, I submit for your consideration the expediency of an appropriation for maintaining a charge' d'affaires near each of those new States. It does not admit of doubt that important commercial advantages might be secured by favorable treaties with them.

The operations of the Treasury during the period which has elapsed since your adjournment have been conducted with signal success. The patriotism of the people has placed at the disposal of the Government the large means demanded by the public exigencies. Much of the national loan has been taken by citizens of the industrial classes, whose confidence in their country's faith and zeal for their country's deliverance from present peril have induced them to contribute to the support of the Government the whole of their limited acquisitions. This fact imposes peculiar obligations to economy in disbursement and energy in action.

The revenue from all sources, including loans, for the financial year ending on the 30th of June, 1861, was $86,835,900.27, and the expenditures for the same period, including payments on account of the public debt, were $84,578,834.47, leaving a balance in the Treasury on the 1st of July of 52,257,065.80. For the first quarter of the financial year ending on the 30th of September, 1861, the receipts from all sources, including the balance of the 1st of July, were $102,532,509.27, and the expenses $98,239,733.09, leaving a balance on the 1st of October, 1861, of $4,292,776.18.

Estimates for the remaining three quarters of the year and for the financial year 1863, together with his views of ways and means for meeting the demands contemplated by them, will be submitted to Congress by the Secretary of the Treasury. It is gratifying to know that the expenditures made necessary by the rebellion are not beyond the resources of the loyal people, and to believe that the same patriotism which has thus far sustained the Government will continue to sustain it till peace and union shall again bless the land.

I respectfully refer to the report of the Secretary of War for information respecting the numerical strength of the Army and for recommendations having in view an increase of its efficiency and the well-being of the various branches of the service intrusted to his care. It is gratifying to know that the patriotism of the people has proved equal to the occasion, and that the number of troops tendered greatly exceeds the force which Congress authorized me to call into the field.

I refer with pleasure to those portions of his report which make allusion to the creditable degree of discipline already attained by our troops and to the excellent sanitary condition of the entire Army.

The recommendation of the Secretary for an organization of the militia upon a uniform basis is a subject of vital importance to the future safety of the country, and is commended to the serious attention of Congress.

The large addition to the Regular Army, in connection with the defection that has so considerably diminished the number of its officers, gives peculiar importance to his recommendation for increasing the corps of cadets to the greatest capacity of the Military Academy.

By mere omission, I presume, Congress has failed to provide chaplains for hospitals occupied by volunteers. This subject was brought to my notice, and I was induced to draw up the form of a letter, one copy of which, properly addressed, has been delivered to each of the persons, and at the dates respectively named and stated in a schedule, containing also the form of the letter marked A, and herewith transmitted.

These gentlemen, I understand, entered upon the duties designated at the times respectively stated in the schedule, and have labored faithfully therein ever since. I therefore recommend that they be compensated at the same rate as chaplains in the Army. I further suggest that general provision be made for chaplains to serve at hospitals, as well as with regiments.

The report of the Secretary of the Navy presents in detail the operations of that branch of the service, the activity and energy which have characterized its administration, and the results of measures to increase its efficiency and power. Such have been the additions, by construction and purchase, that it may almost be said a navy has been created and brought into service since our difficulties commenced.

Besides blockading our extensive coast, squadrons larger than ever before assembled under our flag have been put afloat and performed deeds which have increased our naval renown.

I would invite special attention to the recommendation of the Secretary for a more perfect organization of the Navy by introducing additional grades in the service.

The present organization is defective and unsatisfactory, and the suggestions submitted by the Department will, it is believed, if adopted, obviate the difficulties alluded to, promote harmony, and increase the efficiency of the Navy.

There are three vacancies on the bench of the Supreme Court—two by the decease of Justices Daniel and McLean and one by the resignation of Justice Campbell. I have so far forborne making nominations to fill these vacancies for reasons which I will now state. Two of the outgoing judges resided within the States now overrun by revolt, so that if successors were appointed in the same localities they could not now serve upon their circuits; and many of the most competent men there probably would not take the personal hazard of accepting to serve, even here, upon the Supreme bench. I have been unwilling to throw all the appointments northward, thus disabling myself from doing justice to the South on the return of peace; although I may remark that to transfer to the North one which has heretofore been in the South would not, with reference to territory and population, be unjust.

During the long and brilliant judicial career of Judge McLean his circuit grew into an empire altogether too large for any one judge to give the courts therein more than a nominal attendance—rising in population from 1,470,018 in 1830 to 6,151,405 in 1860.

Besides this, the country generally has outgrown our present judicial system. If uniformity was at all intended, the system requires that all the States shall be accommodated with circuit courts, attended by Supreme judges, while, in fact, Wisconsin, Minnesota, Iowa, Kansas, Florida, Texas, California, and Oregon have never had any such courts. Nor can this well be remedied without a change in the system, because the adding of judges to the Supreme Court, enough for the accommodation of all parts of the country with circuit courts, would create a court altogether too numerous for a judicial body of any sort. And the evil, if it be one, will increase as new States come into the Union. Circuit courts are useful or they are not useful. If useful, no State should be denied them; if not useful, no State should have them. Let them be provided for all or abolished as to all.

Three modifications occur to me, either of which, I think, would be an improvement upon our present system. Let the Supreme Court be of convenient number in every event; then, first, let the whole country be divided into circuits of convenient size, the Supreme judges to serve in a number of them corresponding to their own number, and independent circuit judges be provided for all the rest; or, secondly, let the Supreme judges be relieved from circuit duties and circuit judges provided for all the circuits; or, thirdly, dispense with circuit courts altogether, leaving the judicial functions wholly to the district courts and an independent Supreme Court.

I respectfully recommend to the consideration of Congress the present condition of the statute laws, with the hope that Congress will be able to find an easy remedy for many of the inconveniences and evils which constantly embarrass those engaged in the practical administration of them. Since the organization of the Government Congress has enacted some 5,000 acts and joint resolutions, which fill more than 6,000 closely printed pages and are scattered through many volumes. Many of these acts have been drawn in haste and without sufficient caution, so that their provisions are often obscure in themselves or in conflict with each other, or at least so doubtful as to render it very difficult for even the best-informed persons to ascertain precisely what the statute law really is.

It seems to me very important that the statute laws should be made as plain and intelligible as possible, and be reduced to as small a compass as may consist with the fullness and precision of the will of the Legislature and the perspicuity of its language. This well done would, I think, greatly facilitate the labors of those whose duty it is to assist in the administration of the laws, and would be a lasting benefit to the people, by placing before them in a more accessible and intelligible form the laws which so deeply concern their interests and their duties.

I am informed by some whose opinions I respect that all the acts of Congress now in force and of a permanent and general nature might be revised and rewritten so as to be embraced in one volume (or at most two volumes) of ordinary and convenient size; and I respectfully recommend to Congress to consider of the subject, and if my suggestion be approved to devise such plan as to their wisdom shall seem most proper for the attainment of the end proposed.

One of the unavoidable consequences of the present insurrection is the entire suppression in many places of all the ordinary means of administering civil justice by the officers and in the forms of existing law. This is the case, in whole or in part, in all the insurgent States; and as our armies advance upon and take possession of parts of those States the practical evil becomes more apparent. There are no courts nor officers to whom the citizens of other States may apply for the enforcement of their lawful claims against citizens of the insurgent States, and there is a vast amount of debt constituting such claims. Some have estimated it as high as $200,000,000, due in large part from insurgents in open rebellion to loyal citizens who are even now making great sacrifices in the discharge of their patriotic duty to support the Government.

Under these circumstances I have been urgently solicited to establish by military power courts to administer summary justice in such cases I have thus far declined to do it, not because I had any doubt that the end proposed—the collection of the debts—was just and right in itself, but because I have been unwilling to go beyond the pressure of necessity in the unusual exercise of power. But the powers of Congress, I suppose, are equal to the anomalous occasion, and therefore I refer the whole matter to Congress, with the hope that a plan may be devised for the administration of justice in all such parts of the insurgent States and Territories as may be under the control of this Government, whether by a voluntary return to allegiance and order or by the power of our arms; this, however, not to be a permanent institution, but a temporary substitute, and to cease as soon as the ordinay courts can be reestablished in peace.

It is important that some more convenient means should be provided, if possible, for the adjustment of claims against the Government, especially in view of their increased number by reason of the war. It is as much the duty of Government to render prompt justice against itself in favor of citizens as it is to administer the same between private individuals. The investigation and adjudication of claims in their nature belong to the judicial department. Besides, it is apparent that the attention of Congress will be more than usually engaged for some time to come with great national questions. It was intended by the organization of the Court of Claims mainly to remove this branch of business from the halls of Congress: but while the court has proved to be an effective and valuable means of investigation, it in great degree fails to effect the object of its creation for want of power to make its judgments final.

Fully aware of the delicacy, not to say the danger, of the subject, I commend to your careful consideration whether this power of making judgments final may not properly be given to the court, reserving the right of appeal on questions of law to the Supreme Court, with such other provisions as experience may have shown to be necessary.

I ask attention to the report of the Postmaster-General, the following being a summary statement of the condition of the Department:

The revenue from all sources during the fiscal year ending June 30, 1861, including the annual permanent appropriation of $700,000 for the transportation of "free mail matter," was $9,049,296.40, being about 2 per cent less than the revenue for 1860.

The expenditures were $13,606,759.11, showing a decrease of more than 8 per cent as compared with those of the previous year and leaving an excess of expenditure over the revenue for the last fiscal year of $4,557,462.71.

The gross revenue for the year ending June 30, 1863, is estimated at an increase of 4 per cent on that of 1861, making $8,683,000, to which should be added the earnings of the Department in carrying free matter, viz, $700,000, making $9,383,000.

The total expenditures for 1863 are estimated at $12,528,000, leaving an estimated deficiency of $3,145,000 to be supplied from the Treasury in addition to the permanent appropriation.

The present insurrection shows, I think, that the extension of this District across the Potomac River at the time of establishing the capital here was eminently wise, and consequently that the relinquishment of that portion of it which lies within the State of

Virginia was unwise and dangerous. I submit for your consideration the expediency of regaining that part of the District and the restoration of the original boundaries thereof through negotiations with the State of Virginia.

The report of the Secretary of the Interior, with the accompanying documents, exhibits the condition of the several branches of the public business pertaining to that Department. The depressing influences of the insurrection have been specially felt in the operations of the Patent and General Land Offices. The cash receipts from the sales of public lands during the past year have exceeded the expenses of our land system only about $200,000. The sales have been entirely suspended in the Southern States, while the interruptions to the business of the country and the diversion of large numbers of men from labor to military service have obstructed settlements in the new States and Territories of the Northwest.

The receipts of the Patent Office have declined in nine months about $100,000, rendering a large reduction of the force employed necessary to make it self-sustaining.

The demands upon the Pension Office will be largely increased by the insurrection. Numerous applications for pensions, based upon the casualties of the existing war, have already been made. There is reason to believe that many who are now upon the pension rolls and in receipt of the bounty of the Government are in the ranks of the insurgent army or giving them aid and comfort. The Secretary of the Interior has directed a suspension of the payment of the pensions of such persons upon proof of their disloyalty. I recommend that Congress authorize that officer to cause the names of such persons to be stricken from the pension rolls.

The relations of the Government with the Indian tribes have been greatly disturbed by the insurrection, especially in the southern superintendency and in that of New Mexico. The Indian country south of Kansas is in the possession of insurgents from Texas and Arkansas. The agents of the United States appointed since the 4th of March for this superintendency have been unable to reach their posts, while the most of those who were in office before that time have espoused the insurrectionary cause, and assume to exercise the powers of agents by virtue of commissions from the insurrectionists. It has been stated in the public press that a portion of those Indians have been organized as a military force and are attached to the army of the insurgents. Although the Government has no official information upon this subject, letters have been written to the Commissioner of Indian Affairs by several prominent chiefs giving assurance of their loyalty to the United States and expressing a wish for the presence of Federal troops to protect them. It is believed that upon the repossession of the country by the Federal forces the Indians will readily cease all hostile demonstrations and resume their former relations to the Government.

Agriculture, confessedly the largest interest of the nation, has not a department nor a bureau, but a clerkship only, assigned to it in the Government. While it is fortunate that this great interest is so independent in its nature as to not have demanded and extorted more from the Government, I respectfully ask Congress to consider whether something more cannot be given voluntarily with general advantage.

Annual reports exhibiting the condition of our agriculture, commerce, and manufactures would present a fund of information of great practical value to the country. While I make no suggestion as to details, I venture the opinion that an agricultural and statistical bureau might profitably be organized.

The execution of the laws for the suppression of the African slave trade has been confided to the Department of the Interior. It is a subject of gratulation that the efforts which have been made for the suppression of this inhuman traffic have been recently attended with unusual success. Five vessels being fitted out for the slave trade have been seized and condemned. Two mates of vessels engaged in the trade and one person in equipping a vessel as a slaver have been convicted and subjected to the penalty of fine and imprisonment, and one captain, taken with a cargo of Africans on board his vessel, has been convicted of the highest grade of offense under our laws, the punishment of which is death.

The Territories of Colorado, Dakota, and Nevada, created by the last Congress, have been organized, and civil administration has been inaugurated therein under auspices especially gratifying when it is considered that the leaven of treason was found existing in some of these new countries when the Federal officers arrived there.

The abundant natural resources of these Territories, with the security and protection afforded by organized government, will doubtless invite to them a large immigration when peace shall restore the business of the country to its accustomed channels. I submit the resolutions of the legislature of Colorado, which evidence the patriotic spirit of the people of the Territory. So far the authority of the United States has been upheld in all the Territories, as it is hoped it will be in the future. I commend their interests and defense to the enlightened and generous care of Congress.

I recommend to the favorable consideration of Congress the interests of the District of Columbia. The insurrection has been the cause of much suffering and sacrifice to its inhabitants, and as they have no representative in Congress that body should not overlook their just claims upon the Government.

At your late session a joint resolution was adopted authorizing the President to take measures for facilitating a proper representation of the industrial interests of the United States at the exhibition of the industry of all nations to be holden at London in the year 1862. I regret to say I have been unable to give personal attention to this subject—a subject at once so interesting in itself and so extensively and intimately connected with the material prosperity of the world. Through the Secretaries of State and of the Interior a plan or system has been devised and partly matured, and which will be laid before you.

Under and by virtue of the act of Congress entitled "An act to confiscate property used for insurrectionary purposes," approved August 6, 1861, the legal claims of certain persons to the labor and service of certain other persons have become forfeited, and numbers of the latter thus liberated are already dependent on the United States and must be provided for in some way. Besides this, it is not impossible that some of the States will pass similar enactments for their own benefit respectively, and by operation of which persons of the same class will be thrown upon them for disposal. In such case I recommend that Congress provide for accepting such persons from such States, according to some mode of valuation, in lieu, pro tanto, of direct taxes, or upon some other plan to be agreed on with such States respectively; that such persons, on such acceptance by the General Government, be at once deemed free, and that in any event steps be taken for colonizing both classes (or the one first mentioned if the other shall not be brought into existence) at some place or places in a climate congenial to them. It might be well to consider, too, whether the free colored people already in the United States could not, so far as individuals may desire, be included in such colonization.

To carry out the plan of colonization may involve the acquiring of territory, and also the appropriation of money beyond that to be expended in the territorial acquisition. Having practiced the acquisition of territory for nearly sixty years, the question of constitutional power to do so is no longer an open one with us. The power was questioned at first by Mr. Jefferson, who, however, in the purchase of Louisiana, yielded his scruples on the plea of great expediency. If it be said that the only legitimate object of acquiring territory is to furnish homes for white men, this measure effects that object, for the emigration of colored men leaves additional room for white men remaining or coming here. Mr. Jefferson, however, placed the importance of procuring Louisiana more on political and commercial grounds than on providing room for population.

On this whole proposition, including the appropriation of money with the acquisition of territory, does not the expediency amount to absolute necessity—that without which the Government itself cannot be perpetuated?

The war continues. In considering the policy to be adopted for suppressing the insurrection I have been anxious and careful that the inevitable conflict for this purpose shall not degenerate into a violent and remorseless revolutionary struggle. I have therefore in every case thought it proper to keep the integrity of the Union prominent as the primary object of the contest on our pan, leaving all questions which are not of vital military importance to the more deliberate action of the Legislature.

In the exercise of my best discretion I have adhered to the blockade of the ports held by the insurgents, instead of putting in force by proclamation the law of Congress enacted .at the late session for closing those ports.

So also, obeying the dictates of prudence, as well as the obligations of law, instead of transcending I have adhered to the act of Congress to confiscate property used for insurrectionary purposes. If a new law upon the same subject shall be proposed, its propriety will be duly considered. The Union must be preserved, and hence all indispensable means must be employed. We should not be in haste to determine that radical and extreme measures, which may reach the loyal as well as the disloyal, are indispensable.

The inaugural address at the beginning of the Administration and the message to Congress at the late special session were both mainly devoted to the domestic controversy out of which the insurrection and consequent war have sprung. Nothing now occurs to add or subtract to or from the principles or general purposes stated and expressed in those documents.

The last ray of hope for preserving the Union peaceably expired at the assault upon Fort Sumter, and a general review of what has occurred since may not be unprofitable. What was painfully uncertain then is much better defined and more distinct now, and the progress of events is plainly in the right direction. The insurgents confidently claimed a strong support from north of Mason and Dixon's line, and the friends of the Union were not free from apprehension on the point. This, however, was soon settled definitely, and on the right side. South of the line noble little Delaware led off right from the first. Maryland was made to seem against the Union. Our soldiers were assaulted, bridges were burned, and railroads torn up within her limits, and we were many days at one time without the ability to bring a single regiment over her soil to the capital. Now her bridges and railroads are repaired and open to the Government; she already gives seven regiments to the cause of the Union, and none to the enemy; and her people, at a regular election, have sustained the Union by a larger majority and a larger aggregate vote than they ever before gave to any candidate or any question. Kentucky, too, for some time in doubt, is now decidedly and, I think, unchangeably ranged on the side of the Union. Missouri is comparatively quiet, and, I believe, cannot again be overrun by the insurrectionists. These three States of Maryland, Kentucky, and Missouri, neither of which would promise a single soldier at first, have now an aggregate of not less than 40,000 in the field for the Union, while of their citizens certainly not more than a third of that number, and they of doubtful whereabouts and doubtful existence, are in arms against us. After a somewhat bloody struggle of months, winter closes on the Union people of western Virginia, leaving them masters of their own country.

An insurgent force of about 1,500, for months dominating the narrow peninsular region constituting the counties of Accomac and Northampton, and known as Eastern Shore of Virginia, together with some contiguous parts of Maryland, have laid down their arms, and the people there have renewed their allegiance to and accepted the protection of the old flag. This leaves no armed insurrectionist north of the Potomac or east of the Chesapeake.

Also we have obtained a footing at each of the isolated points on the southern coast of Hatteras, Port Royal, Tybee Island (near Savannah), and Ship Island; and we likewise have some general accounts of popular movements in behalf of the Union in North Carolina and Tennessee.

These things demonstrate that the cause of the Union is advancing steadily and certainly southward.

Since your last adjournment Lieutenant-General Scott has retired from the head of the Army. During his long life the nation has not been unmindful of his merit; yet on calling to mind how faithfully, ably, and brilliantly he has served the country, from a time far back in our history, when few of the now living had been born, and thenceforward continually, I cannot but think we are still his debtors. I submit, therefore, for your consideration what further mark of recognition is due to him, and to ourselves as a grateful people.

With the retirement of General Scott came the Executive duty of appointing in his stead a General in Chief of the Army. It is a fortunate circumstance that neither in council nor country was there, so far as I know, any difference of opinion as to the proper person to be selected. The retiring chief repeatedly expressed his judgment in favor of General McClellan for the position, and in this the nation seemed to give a unanimous concurrence. The designation of General McClellan is therefore in considerable degree the selection of the country as well as of the Executive, and hence there is better reason to hope there will be given him the confidence and cordial support thus by fair implication promised, and without which he cannot with so full efficiency serve the country.

It has been said that one bad general is better than two good ones, and the saying is true if taken to mean no more than that an army is better directed by a single mind, though inferior, than by two superior ones at variance and cross-purposes with each other.

And the same is true in all joint operations wherein those engaged can have none but a common end in view and can differ only as to the choice of means. In a storm at sea no one on board can wish the ship to sink, and yet not unfrequently all go down together because too many will direct and no single mind can be allowed to control.

It continues to develop that the insurrection is largely, if not exclusively, a war upon the first principle of popular government— the rights of the people. Conclusive evidence of this is found in the most grave and maturely considered public documents, as well as in the general tone of the insurgents. In those documents we find the abridgment of the existing right of suffrage and the denial to the people of all right to participate in the selection of public officers except the legislative boldly advocated, with labored arguments to prove that large control of the people in government is the source of all political evil. Monarchy itself is sometimes hinted at as a possible refuge from the power of the people.

In my present position I could scarcely be justified were I to omit raising a warning voice against this approach of returning despotism.

It is not needed nor fitting here that a general argument should be made in favor of popular institutions, but there is one point, with its connections, not so hackneyed as most others, to which I ask a brief attention. It is the effort to place capital on an equal footing with, if not above, labor in the structure of government. It is assumed that labor is available only in connection with capital; that nobody labors unless somebody else, owning capital, somehow by the use of it induces him to labor. This assumed, it is next considered whether it is best that capital shall hire laborers, and thus induce them to work by their own consent, or buy them and drive them to it without their consent. Having proceeded so far, it is naturally concluded that all laborers are either hired laborers or what we call slaves. And further, it is assumed that whoever is once a hired laborer is fixed in that condition for life.

Now there is no such relation between capital and labor as assumed, nor is there any such thing as a free man being fixed for life in the condition of a hired laborer. Both these assumptions are false, and all inferences from them are groundless.

Labor is prior to and independent of capital. Capital is only the fruit of labor, and could never have existed if labor had not first existed. Labor is the superior of capital, and deserves much the higher consideration. Capital has its rights, which are as worthy of protection as any other rights. Nor is it denied that there is, and probably always will be, a relation between labor and capital producing mutual benefits. The error is in assuming that the whole labor of community exists within that relation. A few men own capital, and that few avoid labor themselves, and with their capital hire or buy another few to labor for them. A large majority belong to neither class—neither work for others nor have others working for them. In most of the Southern States a majority of the whole people of all colors are neither slaves nor masters, while in the Northern a large majority are neither hirers nor hired. Men, with their families—wives, sons, and daughters—work for themselves on their farms, in their houses, and in their shops, taking the whole product to themselves, and asking no favors of capital on the one hand nor of hired laborers or slaves on the other. It is not forgotten that a considerable number of persons mingle their own labor with capital; that is, they labor with their own hands and also buy or hire others to labor for them; but this is only a mixed and not a distinct class. No principle stated is disturbed by the existence of this mixed class.

Again, as has already been said, there is not of necessity any such thing as the free hired laborer being fixed to that condition for life. Many independent men everywhere in these States a few years back in their lives were hired laborers. The prudent, penniless beginner in the world labors for wages awhile, saves a surplus with which to buy tools or land for himself, then labors on his own account another while, and at length hires another new beginner to help him. This is the just and generous and prosperous system which opens the way to all, gives hope to all, and consequent energy and progress and improvement of condition to all. No men living are more worthy to be trusted than those who toil up from poverty; none less inclined to take or touch aught which they have not honestly earned. Let them beware of surrendering a political power which they already possess, and which if surrendered will surely be used to close the door of advancement against such as they and to fix new disabilities and burdens upon them till all of liberty shall be lost.

From the first taking of our national census to the last are seventy years, and we find our population at the end of the period eight times as great as it was at the beginning. The increase of those other things which men deem desirable has been even greater. We thus have at one view what the popular principle, applied to Government through the machiney, of the States and the Union, has produced in a given time, and also what if firmly maintained it promises for the future. There are already among us those who if the Union be preserved will live to see it contain 250,000,000. The struggle of to-day is not altogether for to-day; it is for a vast future also. With a reliance on Providence all the more firm and earnest, let us proceed in the great task which events have devolved upon us.

SECOND STATE OF THE UNION ADDRESS (1862)

Fellow-Citizens of the Senate and House of Representatives:

Since your last annual assembling another year of health and bountiful harvests has passed, and while it has not pleased the Almighty to bless us with a return of peace, we can but press on, guided by the best light He gives us, trusting that in His own good time and wise way all will yet be well.

The correspondence touching foreign affairs which has taken place during the last year is herewith submitted, in virtual compliance with a request to that effect made by the House of Representatives near the close of the last session of Congress. If the condition of our relations with other nations is less gratifying than it has usually been at former periods, it is certainly more satisfactory than a nation so unhappily distracted as we are might reasonably have apprehended. In the month of June last there were some grounds to expect that the maritime powers which at the beginning of our domestic difficulties so unwisely and unnecessarily, as we think, recognized the insurgents as a belligerent would soon recede from that position, which has proved only less injurious to themselves than to our own country. But the temporary reverses which afterwards befell the national arms, and which were exaggerated by our own disloyal citizens abroad, have hitherto delayed that act of simple justice.

The civil war, which has so radically changed for the moment the occupations and habits of the American people, has necessarily disturbed the social condition and affected very deeply the prosperity of the nations with which we have carried on a commerce that has been steadily increasing throughout a period of half a century. It has at the same time excited political ambitions and apprehensions which have produced a profound agitation throughout the civilized world. In this unusual agitation we have forborne from taking part in any controversy between foreign states and between parties or factions in such states. We have attempted no propagandism and acknowledged no revolution. But we have left to every nation the exclusive conduct and management of its own affairs. Our struggle has been, of course, contemplated by foreign nations with reference less to its own merits than to its supposed and often exaggerated effects and consequences resulting to those nations themselves. Nevertheless, complaint on the part of this Government, even if it were just, would certainly be unwise. The treaty with Great Britain for the suppression of the slave trade has been put into operation with a good prospect of complete success. It is an occasion of special pleasure to acknowledge that the execution of it on the part of Her Majesty's Government has been marked with a jealous respect for the authority of the United States and the rights of their moral and loyal citizens.

The convention with Hanover for the abolition of the Stade dues has been carried into full effect under the act of Congress for that purpose. A blockade of 3,000 miles of seacoast could not be established and vigorously enforced in a season of great commercial activity like the present without committing occasional mistakes and inflicting unintentional injuries upon foreign nations and their subjects. A civil war occurring in a country, where foreigners reside and carry on trade under treaty stipulations is necessarily fruitful of complaints of the violation of neutral rights. All such collisions tend to excite misapprehensions, and possibly to produce mutual reclamations between nations which have a common interest in preserving peace and friendship. In clear cases of these kinds I have so far as possible heard and redressed complaints which have been presented by friendly powers. There is still, however, a large and an augmenting number of doubtful cases upon which the Government is unable to agree with the governments whose protection is demanded by the claimants. There are, moreover, many cases in which the United States or their citizens suffer wrongs from the naval or military authorities of foreign nations which the governments of those states are not at once prepared to redress. I have proposed to some of the foreign states thus interested mutual conventions to examine and adjust such complaints. This proposition has been made especially to

Great Britain, to France, to Spain, and to Prussia. In each case it has been kindly received, but has not yet been formally adopted.

I deem it my duty to recommend an appropriation in behalf of the owners of the Norwegian bark Admiral P. Tordenskiold, which vessel was in May, 1861, prevented by the commander of the blockading force off Charleston from leaving that port with cargo, notwithstanding a similar privilege had shortly before been granted to an English vessel. I have directed the Secretary of State to cause the papers in the case to be communicated to the proper committees.

Applications have been made to me by many free Americans of African descent to favor their emigration, with a view to such colonization as was contemplated in recent acts of Congress. Other parties, at home and abroad—some from interested motives, others upon patriotic considerations, and still others influenced by philanthropic sentiments—have suggested similar measures, while, on the other hand, several of the Spanish American Republics have protested against the sending of such colonies to their respective territories. Under these circumstances I have declined to move any such colony to any state without first obtaining the consent of its government, with an agreement on its part to receive and protect such emigrants in all the rights of freemen; and I have at the same time offered to the several States situated within the Tropics, or having colonies there, to negotiate with them, subject to the advice and consent of the Senate, to favor the voluntary emigration of persons of that class to their respective territories, upon conditions which shall be equal, just, and humane. Liberia and Hayti are as yet the only countries to which colonists of African descent from here could go with certainty of being received and adopted as citizens; and I regret to say such persons contemplating colonization do not seem so willing to migrate to those countries as to some others, nor so willing as I think their interest demands. I believe, however, opinion among them in this respect is improving, and that ere long there will be an augmented and considerable migration to both these countries from the United States.

The new commercial treaty between the United States and the Sultan of Turkey has been carried into execution.

A commercial and consular treaty has been negotiated, subject to the Senate's consent, with Liberia, and a similar negotiation is now pending with the Republic of Hayti. A considerable improvement of the national commerce is expected to result from these measures. Our relations with Great Britain, France, Spain, Portugal, Russia, Prussia, Denmark, Sweden, Austria, the Netherlands, Italy, Rome, and the other European States remain undisturbed. Very favorable relations also continue to be maintained with Turkey, Morocco, China, and Japan.

During the last year there has not only been no change of our previous relations with the independent States of our own continent, but more friendly sentiments than have heretofore existed are believed to be entertained by these neighbors, whose safety and progress are so intimately connected with our own. This statement especially applies to Mexico, Nicaragua, Costa Rica, Honduras, Peru, and Chile. The commission under the convention with the Republic of New Granada closed its session without having audited and passed upon all the claims which were submitted to it. A proposition is pending to revive the convention, that it may be able to do more complete justice. The joint commission between the United States and the Republic of Costa Rica has completed its labors and submitted its report. I have favored the project for connecting the United States with Europe by an Atlantic telegraph, and a similar project to extend the telegraph from San Francisco to connect by a Pacific telegraph with the line which is being extended across the Russian Empire. The Territories of the United States, with unimportant exceptions have remained undisturbed by the civil war; and they are exhibiting such evidence of prosperity as justifies an expectation that some of them will soon be in a condition to be organized as States and be constitutionally admitted into the Federal Union.

The immense mineral resources of some of those Territories ought to be developed as rapidly as possible. Every step in that direction would have a tendency to improve the revenues of the Government and diminish the burdens of the people. It is worthy of your serious consideration whether some extraordinary measures to promote that end cannot be adopted. The means which suggests itself as most likely to be effective is a scientific exploration of the mineral regions in those Territories with a view to the publication of its results at home and in foreign countries—results which cannot fail to be auspicious.

The condition of the finances will claim your most diligent consideration. The vast expenditures incident to the military and naval operations required for the suppression of the rebellion have hitherto been met with a promptitude and certainty unusual in similar circumstances, and the public credit has been fully maintained. The continuance of the war, however, and the increased disbursements made necessary by the augmented forces now in the field demand your best reflections as to the best modes of providing the necessary revenue without injury to business and with the least possible burdens upon labor.

The suspension of specie payments by the banks soon after the commencement of your last session made large issues of United States notes unavoidable. In no other way could the payment of the troops and the satisfaction of other just demands be so economically or so well provided for. The judicious legislation of Congress, securing the receivability of these notes for loans and internal duties and making them a legal tender for other debts, has made them an universal currency, and has satisfied, partially at least, and for the time, the long-felt want of an uniform circulating medium, saving thereby to the people immense sums in discounts and exchanges.

A return to specie payments, however, at the earliest period compatible with due regard to all interests concerned should ever be kept in view. Fluctuations in the value of currency are always injurious, and to reduce these fluctuations to the lowest possible point will always be a leading purpose in wise legislation. Convertibility, prompt and certain convertibility, into coin is generally acknowledged to be the best and surest safeguard against them; and it is extremely doubtful whether a circulation of United States notes payable in coin and sufficiently large for the wants of the people can be permanently, usefully, and safely maintained.

Is there, then, any other mode in which the necessary provision for the public wants can be made and the great advantages of a safe and uniform currency secured?

I know of none which promises so certain results and is at the same time so unobjectionable as the organization of banking associations, under a general act of Congress, well guarded in its provisions. To such associations the Government might furnish circulating notes, on the security of United States bonds deposited in the Treasury. These notes, prepared under the supervision of proper officers, being uniform in appearance and security and convertible always into coin, would at once protect labor against the evils of a vicious currency and facilitate commerce by cheap and safe exchanges.

A moderate reservation from the interest on the bonds would compensate the United States for the preparation and distribution of the notes and a general supervision of the system, and would lighten the burden of that part of the public debt employed as securities. The public credit, moreover, would be greatly improved and the negotiation of new loans greatly facilitated by the steady market demand for Government bonds which the adoption of the proposed system would create. It is an additional recommendation of the measure, of considerable weight, in my judgment, that it would reconcile as far as possible all existing interests by the opportunity offered to existing institutions to reorganize under the act, substituting only the secured uniform national circulation for the local and various circulation, secured and unsecured, now issued by them.

The receipts into the treasury from all sources, including loans and balance from the preceding year, for the fiscal year ending on the 30th June, 1862, were $583,885,247.06, of which sum $49,056,397.62 were derived from customs; $1,795,331.73 from the direct tax; from public lands, $152,203.77; from miscellaneous sources, $931,787.64; from loans in all forms, $529,692,460.50. The remainder, :$2,257,065.80, was the balance from last year.

The disbursements during the same period were: For Congressional, executive, and judicial purposes, $5,939.009.29; for foreign intercourse, $1,339,710.35; for miscellaneous expenses, including the mints, loans, Post-Office deficiencies, collection of revenue, and other like charges, $14,129,771.50; for expenses under the Interior Department, 985.52; under the War Department, $394,368,407.36; under the Navy Department, $42,674,569.69; for interest on public debt, $13,190,324.45; and for payment of public debt, including reimbursement of temporary loan and redemptions, $96,096,922.09; making an aggregate of $570,841,700.25, and leaving a balance in the Treasury on the 1st day of July, 1862, of $13,043,546.81.

It should be observed that the sum of $96,096,922.09, expended for reimbursements and redemption of public debt, being included also in the loans made, may be properly deducted both from receipts and expenditures, leaving the actual receipts for the year $487,788,324.97, and the expenditures $474,744,778.16.

Other information on the subject of the finances will be found in the report of the Secretary of the Treasury, to whose statements and views I invite your most candid and considerate attention.

The reports of the Secretaries of War and of the Navy are herewith transmitted. These reports, though lengthy, are scarcely more than brief abstracts of the very numerous and extensive transactions and operations conducted through those Departments. Nor could I give a summary of them here upon any principle which would admit of its being much shorter than the reports themselves. I therefore content myself with laying the reports before you and asking your attention to them.

It gives me pleasure to report a decided improvement in the financial condition of the Post-Office Department as compared with several preceding years. The receipts for the fiscal year 1861 amounted to $8,349,296.40, which embraced the revenue from all the States of the Union for three quarters of that year. Notwithstanding the cessation of revenue from the so-called seceded States during the last fiscal year, the increase of the correspondence of the loyal States has been sufficient to produce a revenue during the same year of $8,299,820.90, being only $50,000 less than was derived from all the States of the Union during the previous year. The expenditures show a still more favorable result. The amount expended in 1861 was $13,606,759.11. For the last year the amount has been reduced to $11,125,364.13, showing a decrease of about $2,481,000 in the expenditures as compared with the preceding year, and about $3,750,000 as compared with the fiscal year 1860. The deficiency in the Department for the previous year was $4,551,966.98. For the last fiscal year it was reduced to $2,112,814.57. These favorable results are in part owing to the cessation of mail service in the insurrectionary States and in part to a careful review of all expenditures in that Department in the interest of economy. The efficiency of the postal service, it is believed, has also been much improved. The Postmaster-General has also opened a correspondence through the Department of State with foreign governments proposing a convention of postal representatives for the purpose of simplifying the rates of foreign postage and to expedite the foreign mails. This proposition, equally important to our adopted citizens and to the commercial interests of this country, has been favorably entertained and agreed to by all the governments from whom replies have been received.

I ask the attention of Congress to the suggestions of the Postmaster-General in his report respecting the further legislation required, in his opinion, for the benefit of the postal service.

The Secretary of the Interior reports as follows in regard to the public lands:

The public lands have ceased to be a source of revenue. From the 1st July, 1861, to the 30th September, 1862, the entire cash receipts from the sale of lands were $137,476.26—a sum much less than the expenses of our land system during the same period. The homestead law, which will take effect on the 1st of January next, offers such inducements to settlers that sales for cash cannot be expected to an extent sufficient to meet the expenses of the General Land Office and the cost of surveying and bringing the land into market. The discrepancy between the sum here stated as arising from the sales of the public lands and the sum derived from the same source as reported from the Treasury Department arises, as I understand, from the fact that the periods of time, though apparently, were not really coincident at the beginning point, the Treasury report including a considerable sum now which had previously been reported from the Interior, sufficiently large to greatly overreach the sum derived from the three months now reported upon by the Interior and not by the Treasury.

The Indian tribes upon our frontiers have during the past year manifested a spirit of insubordination, and at several points have engaged in open hostilities against the white settlements in their vicinity. The tribes occupying the Indian country south of Kansas renounced their allegiance to the United States and entered into treaties with the insurgents. Those who remained loyal to the United States were driven from the country. The chief of the Cherokees has visited this city for the purpose of restoring the former relations of the tribe with the United States. He alleges that they were constrained by superior force to enter into treaties with the insurgents, and that the United States neglected to furnish the protection which their treaty stipulations required. In the month of August last the Sioux Indians in Minnesota attacked the settlements in their vicinity with extreme ferocity, killing indiscriminately men, women, and children. This attack was wholly unexpected, and therefore no means of defense had been prodded. It is estimated that not less than 800 persons were killed by the Indians, and a large amount of property was destroyed. How this outbreak was induced is not definitely known, and suspicions, which may be unjust, need not to be stated. Information was received by the Indian Bureau from different sources about the time hostilities were commenced that a simultaneous attack was to be made upon the white settlements by all the tribes between the Mississippi River and the Rocky Mountains. The State of Minnesota has suffered great injury from this Indian war. A large portion of her territory has been depopulated, and a severe loss has been sustained by the destruction of property. The people of that State manifest much anxiety for the removal of the tribes beyond the limits of the State as a guaranty against future hostilities. The Commissioner of Indian Affairs will furnish full details. I submit for your especial consideration whether our Indian system shall not be remodeled. Many wise and good men have impressed me with the belief that this can be profitably done.

I submit a statement of the proceedings of commissioners, which shows the progress that has been made in the enterprise of constructing the Pacific Railroad. And this suggests the earliest completion of this road, and also the favorable action of Congress upon the projects now pending before them for enlarging the capacities of the great canals in New York and Illinois, as being of vital and rapidly increasing importance to the whole nation, and especially to the vast interior region hereinafter to be noticed at some greater length. I purpose having prepared and laid before you at an early day some interesting and valuable statistical information upon this subject. The military and commercial importance of enlarging the Illinois and Michigan Canal and improving the Illinois River is presented in the report of Colonel Webster to the Secretary of War, and now transmitted to Congress. I respectfully ask attention to it.

To carry out the provisions of the act of Congress of the 15th of May last, I have caused the Department of Agriculture of the United States to be organized.

The Commissioner informs me that within the period of a few months this Department has established an extensive system of correspondence and exchanges, both at home and abroad, which promises to effect highly beneficial results in the development of a correct knowledge of recent improvements in agriculture, in the introduction of new products, and in the collection of the agricultural statistics of the different States.

Also, that it will soon be prepared to distribute largely seeds, cereals, plants, and cuttings, and has already published and liberally diffused much valuable information in anticipation of a more elaborate report, which will in due time be furnished, embracing some valuable tests in chemical science now in progress in the laboratory.

The creation of this Department was for the more immediate benefit of a large class of our most valuable citizens, and I trust that the liberal basis upon which it has been organized will not only meet your approbation, but that it will realize at no distant day all the fondest anticipations of its most sanguine friends and become the fruitful source of advantage to all our people.

On the 22d day of September last a proclamation was issued by the Executive, a copy of which is herewith submitted. In accordance with the purpose expressed in the second paragraph of that paper, I now respectfully recall your attention to what may be called "compensated emancipation."

A nation may be said to consist of its territory, its people, and its laws. The territory is the only part which is of certain durability. "One generation passeth away and another generation cometh, but the earth abideth forever." It is of the first importance to duly consider and estimate this ever-enduring part. That portion of the earth's surface which is owned and inhabited by the people of the United States is well adapted to be the home of one national family, and it is not well adapted for two or more. Its vast extent and its variety of climate and productions are of advantage in this age for one people, whatever they might have been in former ages. Steam, telegraphs, and intelligence have brought these to be an advantageous combination for one united people.

In the inaugural address I briefly pointed out the total inadequacy of disunion as a remedy for the differences between the people of the two sections. I did so in language which I cannot improve, and which, therefore, I beg to repeat:

One section of our country believes slavery is right and ought to be extended, while the other believes it is wrong and ought not to be extended. This is the only substantial dispute. The fugitive-slave clause of the Constitution and the law for the suppression of the foreign slave trade are each as well enforced, perhaps, as any law can ever be in a community where the moral sense of the people imperfectly supports the law itself. The great body of the people abide by the dry legal obligation in both cases, and a few break over in each. This I think, cannot be perfectly cured, and it would be worse in both cases after the separation of the sections than before. The foreign slave trade, now imperfectly suppressed, would be ultimately revived without restriction in one section, while fugitive slaves, now only partially surrendered, would not be surrendered at all by the other. Physically speaking, we cannot separate. We cannot remove our respective sections from each other nor build an impassable wall between them. A husband and wife may be divorced and go out of the presence and beyond the reach of each other, but the different parts of our country cannot do this. They cannot but remain face to face, and intercourse, either amicable or hostile, must continue between them, Is it possible, then, to make that intercourse more advantageous or more satisfactory after separation than before? Can aliens make treaties easier than friends can make laws? Can treaties be more faithfully enforced between aliens than laws can among friends? Suppose you go to war, you cannot fight always; and when, after much loss on both sides and no gain on either, you cease fighting, the identical old questions, as to terms of intercourse, are again upon you.

There is no line, straight or crooked, suitable for a national boundary upon which to divide. Trace through, from east to west, upon the line between the free and slave country. and we shall find a little more than one-third of its length are rivers, easy to be crossed, and populated, or soon to be populated, thickly upon both sides; while nearly all its remaining length are merely surveyors' lines, over which people may walk back and forth without any consciousness of their presence. No part of this line can be made any more difficult to pass by writing it down on paper or parchment as a national boundary. The fact of separation, if it comes, gives up on the part of the seceding section the fugitive-slave clause, along with all other constitutional obligations upon the section seceded from, while I should expect no treaty stipulation would ever be made to take its place.

But there is another difficulty. The great interior region bounded east by the Alleghanies, north by the British dominions, west by the Rocky Mountains, and south by the line along which the culture of corn and cotton meets, and which includes part of Virginia, part of Tennessee, all of Kentucky, Ohio, Indiana, Michigan, Wisconsin, Illinois,

Missouri, Kansas, Iowa, Minnesota, and the Territories of Dakota, Nebraska, and part of Colorado, already has above 10,000,000 people, and will have 50,000,000 within fifty years if not prevented by any political folly or mistake. It contains more than one-third of the country owned by the United States—certainly more than 1,000,000 square miles. Once half as populous as Massachusetts already is, it would have more than 75,000,000 people. A glance at the map shows that, territorially speaking, it is the great body of the Republic. The other parts are but marginal borders to it. the magnificent region sloping west from the Rocky Mountains to the Pacific being the deepest and also the richest in undeveloped resources. In the production of provisions grains, grasses, and all which proceed from them this great interior region is naturally one of the most important in the world. Ascertain from the statistics the small proportion of the region which has as yet been brought into cultivation, and also the large and rapidly increasing amount of its products, and we shall be overwhelmed with the magnitude of the prospect presented. And yet this region has no seacoast—touches no ocean anywhere. As part of one nation, its people now find, and may forever find, their way to Europe by New York, to South America and Africa by New Orleans, and to Asia by San Francisco; but separate our common country into two nations, as designed by the present rebellion, and every man of this great interior region is thereby cut off from some one or more of these outlets, not perhaps by a physical barrier, but by embarrassing and onerous trade regulations.

And this is true, wherever a dividing or boundary line may be fixed. Place it between the now free and slave country, or place it south of Kentucky or north of Ohio, and still the truth remains that none south of it can trade to any port or place north of it, and none north of it can trade to any port or place south of it, except upon terms dictated by a government foreign to them. These outlets, east, west, and south, are indispensable to the well-being of the people inhabiting and to inhabit this vast interior region. Which of the three may be the best is no proper question. All are better than either, and all of right belong to that people and to their successors forever. True to themselves, they will not ask where a line of separation shall be, but will vow rather that there shall be no such line. Nor are the marginal regions less interested in these communications to and through them to the great outside world. They, too, and each of them, must have access to this Egypt of the West without paying toll at the crossing of any national boundary.

Our national strife springs not from our permanent part; not from the land we inhabit: not from our national homestead. There is no possible severing of this but would multiply and not mitigate evils among us. In all its adaptations and aptitudes it demands union and abhors separation. In fact, it would ere long force reunion, however much of blood and treasure the separation might have cost. Our strife pertains to ourselves—to the passing generations of men—and it can without convulsion be hushed forever with the passing of one generation.

In this view I recommend the adoption of the following resolution and articles amendatory to the Constitution of the United States:

Resolved by the Senate and House of Representatives of the United States of America in Congress assembled (two-thirds of both Houses concurring), That the following articles be proposed to the legislatures (or conventions) of the several States as amendments to the Constitution of the United States, all or any of which articles, when ratified by three-fourths of the said legislatures (or conventions), to be valid as part or parts of the said Constitution, viz:

ART.--. Every State wherein slavery now exists which shall abolish the same therein at any time or times before the 1st day of January., A. D. 1900, shall receive compensation from the United States as follows, to wit:

The President of the United States shall deliver to every such State bonds of the United States bearing interest at the rate of per cent per annum to an amount equal to the aggregate sum of____for each slave shown to have been therein by the Eighth Census of the United States, said bonds to be delivered to such State by installments or in one parcel at the completion of the abolishment, accordingly as the same shall have been gradual or at one time within such State; and interest shall begin to run upon any such bond only from the proper time of its delivery as aforesaid. Any State having received bonds as aforesaid and afterwards reintroducing or tolerating slavery therein shall refund to the United States the bonds so received, or the value thereof, and all interest paid thereon.

ART—All slaves who shall have enjoyed actual freedom by the chances of the war at any time before the end of the rebellion shall be forever free; but all owners of such who shall not have been disloyal shall be compensated for them at the same rates as is provided for States adopting abolishment of slavery, but in such way that no slave shall be twice accounted for.

ART.--Congress may appropriate money and otherwise provide for colonizing free colored persons with their own consent at any place or places without the United States.

I beg indulgence to discuss these proposed articles at some length. Without slavery the rebellion could never have existed; without slavery it could not continue.

Among the friends of the Union there is great diversity of sentiment and of policy in regard to slavery and the African race amongst us. Some would perpetuate slavery; some would abolish it suddenly and without compensation; some would abolish it gradually and with compensation: some would remove the freed people from us, and some would retain them with us; and there are yet other minor diversities. Because of these diversities we waste much strength in struggles among ourselves. By mutual concession we should harmonize and act together. This would be compromise, but it would be compromise among the friends and not with the enemies of the Union. These articles are intended to embody a plan of such mutual concessions. if the plan shall be adopted, it is assumed that emancipation will follow, at least in several of the States.

As to the first article, the main points are, first, the emancipation; secondly, the length of time for consummating it (thirty-seven years); and, thirdly, the compensation.

The emancipation will be unsatisfactory to the advocates of perpetual slavery, but the length of time should greatly mitigate their dissatisfaction. The time spares both races from the evils of sudden derangement—in fact, from the necessity of any derangement—while most of those whose habitual course of thought will be disturbed by the measure will have passed away before its consummation. They will never see it. Another class will hail the prospect of emancipation, but will deprecate the length of time. They will feel that it gives too little to the now living slaves. But it really gives them much. It saves them from the vagrant destitution which must largely attend immediate emancipation in localities where their numbers are very great, and it gives the inspiring assurance that their posterity shall be free forever. The plan leaves to each State choosing to act under it to abolish slavery now or at the end of the century, or at any intermediate time, or by degrees extending over the whole or any part of the period, and it obliges no two States to proceed alike. It also provides for compensation, and generally the mode of making it. This, it would seem, must further mitigate the dissatisfaction of those who favor perpetual slavery, and especially of those who are to receive the compensation. Doubtless some of those who are to pay and not to receive will object. Yet the measure is both just and economical. In a certain sense the liberation of slaves is the destruction of property— property acquired by descent or by purchase, the same as any other property. It is no less true for having been often said that the people of the South are not more responsible for the original introduction of this property than are the people of the North; and when it is remembered how unhesitatingly we all use cotton and sugar and share the profits of dealing in them, it may not be quite safe to say that the South has been more responsible than the North for its continuance. If, then, for a common object this property is to be sacrificed, is it not just that it be done at a common charge?

And if with less money, or money more easily paid, we can preserve the benefits of the Union by this means than we can by the war alone, is it not also economical to do it? Let us consider it, then. Let us ascertain the sum we have expended in the war since compensated emancipation was proposed last March, and consider whether if that measure had been promptly accepted by even some of the slave States the same sum would not have done more to close the war than has been otherwise done. If so, the measure would save money, and in that view would be a prudent and economical measure. Certainly it is not so easy to pay something as it is to pay nothing, but it is easier to pay a large sum than it is to pay a larger one. And it is easier to pay any sum when we are able than it is to pay it before we are able. The war requires large sums, and requires them at once. The aggregate sum necessary for compensated emancipation of course would be large. But it would require no ready cash, nor the bonds even any faster than the emancipation progresses. This might not, and probably would not, close before the end of the thirty-seven years. At that time we shall probably have a hundred millions of people to share the burden, instead of thirty-one millions as now. And not only so, but the increase of our population may be expected to continue for a long time after that period as rapidly as before, because our territory will not have become full. I do not state this inconsiderately. At the same ratio of increase which we have maintained, on an average, from our first national census, in 1790, until that of 1860, we should in 1900 have a population of 103,208,415. And why may we not continue that ratio far beyond that period? Our abundant room, our broad national homestead, is our ample resource. Were our territory as limited as are the British Isles, very certainly our population could not expand as stated. Instead of receiving the foreign born as now, we should be compelled to send part of the native born away. But such is not our condition. We have 2,963,000 square miles. Europe has 3,800,000, with a population averaging 73 1/3 persons to the square mile. Why may not our country at some time average as many? Is it less fertile? Has it more waste surface by mountains, rivers, lakes, deserts, or other causes? Is it inferior to Europe in any natural advantage? If, then, we are at some time to be as populous as Europe, how soon? As to when this may be, we can judge by the past and the present; as to when it will be, if ever, depends much on whether we maintain the Union. Several of our States are already above the average of Europe 73 1/3 to the square mile. Massachusetts has 157; Rhode Island, 133; Connecticut, 99; New York and New Jersey, each 80. Also two other great States, Pennsylvania and Ohio, are not far below, the former having 63 and the latter 59. The States already above the European average, except New York, have increased in as rapid a ratio since passing that point as ever before, while no one of them is equal to some other parts of our country in natural capacity for sustaining a dense population.

Taking the nation in the aggregate, and we find its population and ratio of increase for the several decennial periods to be as follows:

Year	Population	Ratio of increase. Per cent.
1790	3,929,827	....
1800	5,304,937	35.02
1810	7,239,814	36.45
1820	9,638,131	36.45
1830	12,866,020	33.49
1840	17,069,453	32.67
1850	23,191,876	35.87
1860	31,443,790	35.58

This shows an average decennial increase of 34.60 per cent in population through the seventy years from our first to our last census vet taken. It is seen that the ratio of increase at no one of these seven periods is either 2 per cent below or 2 per cent above the average, thus showing how inflexible, and consequently how reliable, the law of increase in our case is. Assuming that it will continue, it gives the following results:

Year	Population
1870	42,323,341
1880	56,967,216
1890	76,677,872

1900	103,208,415
1910	138,918,526
1920	186,984,335
1930	251,680,914

These figures show that our country may be as populous as Europe now is at some point between 1920 and 1930—say about 1925—our territory, at 73 1/3 persons to the square mile, being of capacity to contain 217,186,000.

And we will reach this, too, if we do not ourselves relinquish the chance by the folly and evils of disunion or by long and exhausting war springing from the only great element of national discord among us. While it cannot be foreseen exactly how much one huge example of secession, breeding lesser ones indefinitely, would retard population, civilization, and prosperity, no one can doubt that the extent of it would be very great and injurious.

The proposed emancipation would shorten the war, perpetuate peace, insure this increase of population, and proportionately the wealth of the country. With these we should pay all the emancipation would cost, together with our other debt, easier than we should pay our other debt without it. If we had allowed our old national debt to run at 6 per cent per annum, simple interest, from the end of our revolutionary struggle until to-day, without paying anything on either principal or interest, each man of us would owe less upon that debt now than each man owed upon it then; and this because our increase of men through the whole period has been greater than 6 per cent—has run faster than the interest upon the debt. Thus time alone relieves a debtor nation, so long as its population increases faster than unpaid interest accumulates on its debt.

This fact would be no excuse for delaying payment of what is justly due, but it shows the great importance of time in this connection—the great advantage of a policy by which we shall not have to pay until we number 100,000,000 what by a different policy we would have to pay now, when we number but 31,000,000. In a word, it shows that a dollar will be much harder to pay for the war than will be a dollar for emancipation on the proposed plan. And then the latter will cost no blood, no precious life. It will be a saving of both.

As to the second article, I think it would be impracticable to return to bondage the class of persons therein contemplated. Some of them, doubtless, in the property sense belong to loyal owners, and hence provision is made in this article for compensating such. The third article relates to the future of the freed people. It does not oblige, but merely authorizes Congress to aid in colonizing such as may consent. This ought not to be regarded as objectionable on the one hand or on the other, insomuch as it comes to nothing unless by the mutual consent of the people to be deported and the American voters, through their representatives in Congress.

I cannot make it better known than it already is that I strongly favor colonization; and yet I wish to say there is an objection urged against free colored persons remaining in the country which is largely imaginary, if not sometimes malicious.

It is insisted that their presence would injure and displace white labor and white laborers. If there ever could be a proper time for mere catch arguments, that time surely is not now. In times like the present men should utter nothing for which they would not willingly be responsible through time and in eternity. Is it true, then, that colored people can displace any more white labor by being free than by remaining slaves? If they stay in their old places, they jostle no white laborers; if they leave their old places, they leave them open to white laborers. Logically, there is neither more nor less of it. Emancipation, even without deportation, would probably enhance the wages of white labor, and very surely would not reduce them. Thus the customary amount of labor would still have to be performed—the freed people would surely not do more than their old proportion of it, and very probably for a time would do less, leaving an increased part to white laborers, bringing their labor into greater demand, and consequently enhancing the wages of it. With deportation, even to a limited extent, enhanced wages to white labor is mathematically certain. Labor is like any other commodity in the market—increase the demand for it and you increase the price of it. Reduce the supply of black labor by colonizing the black laborer out of the country, and by precisely so much you increase the demand for and wages of white labor.

But it is dreaded that the freed people will swarm forth and cover the whole land. Are they not already in the land? Will liberation make them any more numerous? Equally distributed among the whites of the whole country, and there would be but one colored to seven whites. Could the one in any way greatly disturb the seven? There are many communities now having more than one free colored person to seven whites and this without any apparent consciousness of evil from it. The District of Columbia and the States of Maryland and Delaware are all in this condition. The District has more than one free colored to six whites, and yet in its frequent petitions to Congress I believe it has never presented the presence of free colored persons as one of its grievances. But why should emancipation South send the free people North? People of any color seldom run unless there be something to run from. Hertofore colored people to some extent have fled North from bondage, and now, perhaps, from both bondage and destitution. But if gradual emancipation and deportation be adopted, they will have neither to flee from. Their old masters will give them wages at least until new laborers can be procured, and the freedmen in turn will gladly give their labor for the wages till new homes can be found for them in congenial climes and with people of their own blood and race. This proposition can be trusted on the mutual interests involved. And in any event, cannot the North decide for itself whether to receive them?

Again, as practice proves more than theory in any case, has there been any irruption of colored people northward because of the abolishment of slavery in this District last spring?

What I have said of the proportion of free colored persons to the whites in the District is from the census of 1860, having no reference to persons called contrabands nor to those made free by the act of Congress abolishing slavery here.

The plan consisting of these articles is recommended, not but that a restoration of the national authority would be accepted without its adoption.

Nor will the war nor proceedings under the proclamation of September 22, 1862, be stayed because of the recommendation of this plan. Its timely adoption, I doubt not, would bring restoration, and thereby stay both.

And notwithstanding this plan, the recommendation that Congress provide by law for compensating any State which may adopt emancipation before this plan shall have been acted upon is hereby earnestly renewed. Such would be only an advance part of the plan, and the same arguments apply to both.

This plan is recommended as a means, not in exclusion of, but additional to, all others for restoring and preserving the national authority throughout the Union. The subject is presented exclusively in its economical aspect. The plan would, I am confident, secure peace more speedily and maintain it more permanently than can be done by force alone, while all it would cost, considering amounts and manner of payment and times of payment, would be easier paid than will be the additional cost of the war if we rely solely upon force. It is much, very much, that it would cost no blood at all.

The plan is proposed as permanent constitutional law. It cannot become such without the concurrence of, first, two-thirds of Congress, and afterwards three-fourths of the States. The requisite three-fourths of the States will necessarily include seven of the slave States. Their concurrence, if obtained, will give assurance of their severally adopting emancipation at no very distant day upon the new constitutional terms. This assurance would end the struggle now and save the Union forever.

I do not forget the gravity which should characterize a paper addressed to the Congress of the nation by the Chief Magistrate of the nation, nor do I forget that some of you are my seniors, nor that many of you have more experience than I in the conduct of public affairs. Yet I trust that in view of the great responsibility resting upon me you will perceive no want of respect to yourselves in any undue earnestness I may seem to display.

Is it doubted, then, that the plan I propose, if adopted, would shorten the war, and thus lessen its expenditure of money and of blood? Is it doubted that it would restore the national authority and national prosperity and perpetuate both indefinitely? Is it doubted that we here—Congress and Executive can secure its adoption? Will not the good people respond to a united and earnest appeal from us? Can we, can they, by any other means so certainly or so speedily assure these vital objects? We can succeed only by concert. It is not "Can any of us imagine better?" but "Can we all do better?" Object whatsoever is possible, still the question recurs, "Can we do better?" The dogmas of the quiet past are inadequate to the stormy present. The occasion is piled high with difficulty, and we must rise with the occasion. As our case is new, so we must think anew and act anew. We must disenthrall ourselves, and then we shall save our country.

Fellow-citizens, we cannot escape history. We of this Congress and this Administration will be remembered in spite of ourselves. No personal significance or insignificance can spare one or another of us. The fiery trial through which we pass will light us down in honor or dishonor to the latest generation. We say we are for the Union. The world will not forget that we say this. We know how to save the Union. The world knows we do know how to save it. We, even we here, hold the power and bear the responsibility. In giving freedom to the slave we assure freedom to the free—honorable alike in what we give and what we preserve. We shall nobly save or meanly lose the last best hope of earth. Other means may succeed; this could not fail. The way is plain, peaceful, generous, just—a way which if followed the world will forever applaud and God must forever bless.

THIRD STATE OF THE UNION ADDRESS (1863)

Fellow-Citizens of the Senate and House of Representatives:

Another year of health and of sufficiently abundant harvests has passed. For these, and especially for the improved condition of our national affairs, our renewed and profoundest gratitude to God is due.

We remain in peace and friendship with foreign powers.

The efforts of disloyal citizens of the United States to involve us in foreign wars to aid an inexcusable insurrection have been unavailing. Her Britannic Majesty's Government, as was justly expected, have exercised their authority to prevent the departure of new hostile expeditions from British ports. The Emperor of France has by a like proceeding promptly vindicated the neutrality which he proclaimed at the beginning of the contest. Questions of great intricacy and importance have arisen out of the blockade and other belligerent operations between the Government and several of the maritime powers, but they have been discussed and, as far as was possible, accommodated in a spirit of frankness, justice, and mutual good will. It is especially gratifying that our prize courts, by the impartiality of their adjudications, have commanded the respect and confidence of maritime powers.

The supplemental treaty between the United States and Great Britain for the suppression of the African slave trade, made on the 17th day of February last, has been duly ratified and carried into execution. It is believed that so far as American ports and American citizens are concerned that inhuman and odious traffic has been brought to an end.

I shall submit for the consideration of the Senate a convention for the adjustment of possessory claims in Washington Territory arising out of the treaty of the 15th June, 1846, between the United States and Great Britain, and which have been the source of some disquiet among the citizens of that now rapidly improving part of the country.

A novel and important question, involving the extent of the maritime jurisdiction of Spain in the waters which surround the island of Cuba, has been debated without reaching an agreement, and it is proposed in an amicable spirit to refer it to the arbitrament of a friendly power. A convention for that purpose will be submitted to the Senate.

I have thought it proper, subject to the approval of the Senate, to concur with the interested commercial powers in an arrangement for the liquidation of the Scheldt dues, upon the principles which have been heretofore adopted in regard to the imposts upon navigation in the waters of Denmark.

The long-pending controversy between this Government and that of Chile touching the seizure at Sitana, in Peru, by Chilean officers, of a large amount in treasure belonging to citizens of the United States has been brought to a close by the award of His Majesty the King of the Belgians, to whose arbitration the question was referred by the parties. The subject was thoroughly and patiently examined by that justly respected magistrate, and although the sum awarded to the claimants may not have been as large as they expected there is no reason to distrust the wisdom of His Majesty's decision. That decision was promptly complied with by Chile when intelligence in regard to it reached that country.

The joint commission under the act of the last session for carrying into effect the convention with Peru on the subject of claims has been organized at Lima, and is engaged in the business intrusted to it.

Difficulties concerning interoceanic transit through Nicaragua are in course of amicable adjustment.

In conformity with principles set forth in my last annual message, I have received a representative from the United States of Colombia, and have accredited a minister to that Republic.

Incidents occurring in the progress of our civil war have forced upon my attention the uncertain state of international questions touching the rights of foreigners in this country and of United States citizens abroad. In regard to some governments these rights are at least partially, defined by treaties. In no instance, however, is it expressly stipulated that in the event of civil war a foreigner residing in this country within the lines of the insurgents is to be exempted from the rule which classes him as a belligerent, in whose behalf the Government or his country cannot expect any privileges or immunities distinct from that character. I regret to say, however, that such claims have been put forward, and in some instances in behalf of foreigners who have lived in the United States the greater part of their lives.

There is reason to believe that many persons born in foreign countries who have declared their intention to become citizens, or who have been fully naturalized, have evaded the military duty required of them by denying the fact and thereby throwing upon the Government the burden of proof. It has been found difficult or impracticable to obtain this proof, from the want of guides to the proper sources of information. These might be supplied by requiring clerks of courts where declarations of intention may be made or naturalizations effected to send periodically lists of the names of the persons naturalized or declaring their intention to become citizens to the Secretary of the Interior, in whose Department those names might be arranged and printed for general information.

There is also reason to believe that foreigners frequently become citizens of the United States for the sole purpose of evading duties imposed by the laws of their native countries, to which on becoming naturalized here they at once repair, and though never returning to the United States they still claim the interposition of this Government as citizens. Many altercations and great prejudices have heretofore arisen out of this abuse. It is therefore submitted to your serious consideration. It might be advisable to fix a limit beyond which no citizen of the United States residing abroad may claim the interposition of his Government.

The right of suffrage has often been assumed and exercised by aliens under pretenses of naturalization, which they have disavowed when drafted into the military service. I submit the expediency of such an amendment of the law as will make the fact of voting an estoppel against any plea of exemption from military service or other civil obligation on the ground of alienage.

In common with other Western powers, our relations with Japan have been brought into serious jeopardy through the perverse opposition of the hereditary aristocracy of the Empire to the enlightened and liberal policy of the Tycoon, designed to bring the country into the society of nations. It is hoped, although not with entire confidence, that these difficulties may be peacefully overcome. I ask your attention to the claim of the minister residing there for the damages he sustained in the destruction by fire of the residence of the legation at Yedo.

Satisfactory arrangements have been made with the Emperor of Russia, which, it is believed, will result in effecting a continuous line of telegraph through that Empire from our Pacific coast.

I recommend to your favorable consideration the subject of an international telegraph across the Atlantic Ocean, and also of a telegraph between this capital and the national forts along the Atlantic seaboard and the Gulf of Mexico. Such communications, established with any reasonable outlay, would be economical as well as effective aids to the diplomatic, military, and naval service.

The consular system of the United States, under the enactments of the last Congress, begins to be self-sustaining, and there is reason to hope that it may become entirely so with the increase of trade which will ensue whenever peace is restored. Our ministers abroad have been faithful in defending American rights. In protecting commercial interests our consuls have necessarily had to encounter increased labors and responsibilities growing out of the war. These they have for the most part met and discharged with zeal and efficiency. This acknowledgment justly includes those consuls who, residing in Morocco, Egypt, Turkey, Japan, China, and other Oriental countries, are charged with complex functions and extraordinary powers.

The condition of the several organized Territories is generally satisfactory, although Indian disturbances in New Mexico have not been entirely suppressed. The mineral resources of Colorado, Nevada,

Idaho, New Mexico, and Arizona are proving far richer than has been heretofore understood. I lay before you a communication on this subject from the governor of New Mexico. I again submit to your consideration the expediency of establishing a system for the encouragement of immigration. Although this source of national wealth and strength is again flowing with greater freedom than for several years before the insurrection occurred, there is still a great deficiency of laborers in every field of industry, especially in agriculture and in our mines, as well of iron and coal as of the precious metals. While the demand for labor is much increased here, tens of thousands of persons, destitute of remunerative occupation, are thronging our foreign consulates and offering to emigrate to the United States if essential, but very cheap, assistance can be afforded them. It is easy to see that under the sharp discipline of civil war the nation is beginning a new life. This noble effort demands the aid and ought to receive the attention and support of the Government.

Injuries unforeseen by the Government and unintended may in some cases have been inflicted on the subjects or citizens of foreign countries, both at sea and on land, by persons in the service of the United States. As this Government expects redress from other powers when similar injuries are inflicted by persons in their service upon citizens of the United States, we must be prepared to do justice to foreigners. If the existing judicial tribunals are inadequate to this purpose, a special court may be authorized, with power to hear and decide such claims of the character referred to as may have arisen under treaties and the public law. Conventions for adjusting the claims by joint commission have been proposed to some governments, but no definitive answer to the proposition has yet been received from any.

In the course of the session I shall probably have occasion to request you to provide indemnification to claimants where decrees of restitution have been rendered and damages awarded by admiralty courts, and in other cases where this Government may be acknowledged to be liable in principle and where the amount of that liability has been ascertained by an informal arbitration.

The proper officers of the Treasury have deemed themselves required by the law of the United States upon the subject to demand a tax upon the incomes of foreign consuls in this country. While such a demand may not in strictness be in derogation of public law, or perhaps of any existing treaty between the United States and a foreign country, the expediency of so far modifying the act as to exempt from tax the income of such consuls as are not citizens of the United States, derived from the emoluments of their office or from property not situated in the United States, is submitted to your serious consideration. I make this suggestion upon the ground that a comity which ought to be reciprocated exempts our consuls in all other countries from taxation to the extent thus indicated. The United States, I think, ought not to be exceptionally illiberal to international trade and commerce.

The operations of the Treasury during the last year have been successfully conducted. The enactment by Congress of a national banking law has proved a valuable support of the public credit and the general legislation in relation to loans has fully answered the expectations of its favorers. Some amendments may be required to perfect existing laws, but no change in their principles or general scope is believed to be needed.

Since these measures have been in operation all demands on the Treasury, including the pay of the Army and Navy, have been promptly met and fully satisfied. No considerable body of troops, it is believed, were ever more amply provided and more liberally and punctually paid, and it may be added that by no people were the burdens incident to a great war ever more cheerfully borne.

The receipts during the year from all sources, including loans and balance in the Treasury at its commencement, were $901,125,674.86, and the aggregate disbursements $895,796,630.65, leaving a balance on the 1st of July, 1863, of $5,329,044.21. Of the receipts there were derived from customs $69,059,642.40, from internal revenue $37,640,787.95, from direct tax $1,485,103.61, from lands $167,617.17, from miscellaneous sources $3,046,615.35, and from loans $776,682,361.57, making the aggregate $901,125,674.86. Of the disbursements there were for the civil service $23,253,922.08, for pensions and Indians $4,216,520.79, for interest on public debt $24,729,846.51, for the War Department $599,298,600.83, for the Navy Department $63,211,105.27, for payment of funded and temporary debt $181,086,635.07, making the aggregate $895,796,630.65 and leaving the balance of $5,329,044.21. But the payment of funded and temporary debt, having been made from moneys borrowed during the year, must be regarded as merely nominal payments and the moneys borrowed to make them as merely nominal receipts, and their amount, $181,086,635.07, should therefore be deducted both from receipts and disbursements. This being done there remains as actual receipts $720,039,039.79 and the actual disbursements $714,709,995.58, leaving the balance as already stated.

The actual receipts and disbursements for the first quarter and the estimated receipts and disbursements for the remaining three quarters of the current fiscal year (1864) will be shown in detail by the report of the Secretary of the Treasury, to which I invite your attention. It is sufficient to say here that it is not believed that actual results will exhibit a state of the finances less favorable to the country than the estimates of that officer heretofore submitted, while it is confidently expected that at the close of the year both disbursements and debt will be found very considerably less than has been anticipated.

The report of the Secretary of War is a document of great interest. It consists of—

1. The military operations of the year, detailed in the report of the General in Chief. 2. The organization of colored persons into the war service. 3. The exchange of prisoners, fully set forth in the letter of General Hitchcock. 4. The operations under the act for enrolling and calling out the national forces, detailed in the report of the Provost-Marshal-General. 5. The organization of the invalid corps, and 6. The operation of the several departments of the Quartermaster-General, Commissary- General, Paymaster-General, Chief of Engineers, Chief of Ordnance, and Surgeon-General.

It has appeared impossible to make a valuable summary of this report, except such as would be too extended for this place, and hence I content myself by asking your careful attention to the report itself.

The duties devolving on the naval branch of the service during the year and throughout the whole of this unhappy contest have been discharged with fidelity and eminent success. The extensive blockade has been constantly increasing in efficiency as the Navy has expanded, yet on so long a line it has so far been impossible to entirely suppress illicit trade. From returns received at the Navy Department it appears that more than 1,000 vessels have been captured since the blockade was instituted, and that the value of prizes already sent in for adjudication amounts to over $13,000,000.

The naval force of the United States consists at this time of 588 vessels completed and in the course of completion, and of these 75 are ironclad or armored steamers. The events of the war give an increased interest and importance to the Navy which will probably extend beyond the war itself.

The armored vessels in our Navy completed and in service, or which are under contract and approaching completion, are believed to exceed in number those of any other power; but while these may be relied upon for harbor defense and coast service, others of greater strength and capacity will be necessary for cruising purposes and to maintain our rightful position on the ocean.

The change that has taken place in naval vessels and naval warfare since the introduction of steam as a motive power for ships of war demands either a corresponding change in some of our existing navy-yards or the establishment of new ones for the construction and necessary repair of modern naval vessels. No inconsiderable embarrassment, delay, and public injury have been experienced from the want of such governmental establishments. The necessity of such a navy-yard, so furnished, at some suitable place upon the Atlantic seaboard has on repeated occasions been brought to the attention of Congress by the Navy Department, and is again presented in the report of the Secretary which accompanies this communication. I think it my duty to invite your special attention to this subject, and also to that of establishing a yard and depot for naval purposes upon one of the Western rivers. A naval force has been created on those interior waters, and under many disadvantages, within little more than two years, exceeding in numbers the whole naval force of the country at the commencement of the present Administration. Satisfactory and important as have been the performances of the heroic men of the Navy at this interesting period, they are scarcely more wonderful than the success of our mechanics and artisans in the production of war vessels, which has created a new form of naval power.

Our country has advantages superior to any other nation in our resources of iron and timber, with inexhaustible quantities of fuel in the immediate vicinity of both, and all available and in close proximity to navigable waters. Without the advantage of public works, the resources of the nation have been developed and its power displayed in the construction of a Navy of such magnitude, which has at the very period of its creation rendered signal service to the Union.

The increase of the number of seamen in the public service from 7,500 men in the spring of 1861 to about 34,000 at the present time has been accomplished without special legislation or extraordinary bounties to promote that increase. It has been found, however, that the operation of the draft, with the high bounties paid for army recruits, is beginning to affect injuriously the naval service, and will, if not corrected, be likely to impair its efficiency by detaching seamen from their proper vocation and inducing them to enter the Army. I therefore respectfully suggest that Congress might aid both the army and naval services by a definite provision on this subject which would at the same time be equitable to the communities more especially interested.

I commend to your consideration the suggestions of the Secretary of the Navy in regard to the policy of fostering and training seamen and also the education of officers and engineers for the naval service. The Naval Academy is rendering signal service in preparing midshipmen for the highly responsible duties which in after life they will be required to perform. In order that the country should not be deprived of the proper quota of educated officers, for which legal provision has been made at the naval school, the vacancies caused by the neglect or omission to make nominations from the States in insurrection have been filled by the Secretary of the Navy. The school is now more full and complete than at any former period, and in every respect entitled to the favorable consideration of Congress.

During the past fiscal year the financial condition of the Post-Office Department has been one of increasing prosperity, and I am gratified in being able to state that the actual postal revenue has nearly equaled the entire expenditures, the latter amounting to $11,314,206.84 and the former to $11,163,789.59, leaving a deficiency of but $150,417.25. In 1860, the year immediately preceding the rebellion, the deficiency amounted to $5,656,705.49, the postal receipts of that year being $2,645,722.19 less than those of 1863. The decrease since 1860 in the annual amount of transportation has been only about 25 per cent, but the annual expenditure on account of the same has been reduced 35 per cent. It is manifest, therefore, that the Post-Office Department may become self-sustaining in a few years, even with the restoration of the whole service.

The international conference of postal delegates from the principal countries of Europe and America, which was called at the suggestion of the Postmaster-General, met at Paris on the 11th of May last and concluded its deliberations on the 8th of June. The principles established by the conference as best adapted to facilitate postal intercourse between nations and as the basis of future postal conventions inaugurate a general system of uniform international charges at reduced rates of postage, andcannot fail to produce beneficial results.

I refer you to the report of the Secretary of the Interior, which is herewith laid before you, for useful and varied information in relation to the public lands, Indian affairs, patents, pensions, and other matters of public concern pertaining to his Department.

The quantity of land disposed of during the last and the first quarter of the present fiscal years was 3,841,549 acres, of which 161,911 acres were sold for cash, 1,456,514 acres were taken up under the homestead law, and the residue disposed of under laws granting lands for military bounties, for railroad and other purposes. It also appears that the sale of the public lands is largely on the increase.

It has long been a cherished opinion of some of our wisest statesmen that the people of the United States had a higher and more enduring interest in the early settlement and substantial cultivation of the public lands than in the amount of direct revenue to be derived from the sale of them. This opinion has had a controlling influence in shaping legislation upon the subject of our national domain. I may cite as evidence of this the liberal measures adopted in reference to actual settlers; the grant to the States of the overflowed lands within their limits, in order to their being reclaimed and rendered fit for cultivation; the grants to railway companies of alternate sections of land upon the contemplated issues of their roads, which when completed will so largely multiply the facilities for reaching our distant possessions. This policy has received its most signal and beneficent illustration in the recent enactment granting homesteads to actual settlers. Since the 1st day of January last the before-mentioned quantity of 1,456,514 acres of land have been taken up under its provisions. This fact and the amount of sales furnish gratifying evidence of increasing settlement upon the public lands, notwithstanding the great struggle in which the energies of the nation have been engaged, and which has required so large a withdrawal of our citizens from their accustomed pursuits. I cordially concur in the recommendation of the Secretary of the Interior suggesting a modification of the act in favor of those engaged in the military and naval service of the United States. I doubt not that Congress will cheerfully adopt such measures as will, without essentially changing the general features of the system, secure to the greatest practicable extent its benefits to those who have left their homes in the defense of the country in this arduous crisis.

I invite your attention to the views of the Secretary as to the propriety of raising by appropriate legislation a revenue from the mineral lands of the United States.

The measures provided at your last session for the removal of certain Indian tribes have been carried into effect. Sundry treaties have been negotiated, which will in due time be submitted for the constitutional action of the Senate. They contain stipulations for extinguishing the possessory rights of the Indians to large and valuable tracts of lands. It is hoped that the effect of these treaties will result in the establishment of permanent friendly relations with such of these tribes as have been brought into frequent and bloody collision with our outlying settlements and emigrants. Sound policy and our imperative duty to these wards of the Government demand our anxious and constant attention to their material well-being, to their progress in the arts of civilization, and, above all, to that moral training which under the blessing of Divine Providence will confer upon them the elevated and sanctifying influences, the hopes and consolations, of the Christian faith. I suggested in my last annual message the propriety of remodeling our Indian system. Subsequent events have satisfied me of its necessity. The details set forth in the report of the Secretary evince the urgent need for immediate legislative action.

I commend the benevolent institutions established or patronized by the Government in this District to your generous and fostering care. The attention of Congress during the last session was engaged to some extent with a proposition for enlarging the water communication between the Mississippi River and the northeastern seaboard, which proposition, however, failed for the time. Since then, upon a call of the greatest respectability, a convention has been held at Chicago upon the same subject, a summary of whose views is contained in a memorial addressed to the President and Congress, and which I now have the honor to lay before you. That this interest is one which ere long will force its own way I do not entertain a doubt, while it is submitted entirely to your wisdom as to what can be done now. Augmented interest is given to this subject by the actual commencement of work upon the Pacific Railroad, under auspices so favorable to rapid progress and completion. The enlarged navigation becomes a palpable need to the great road.

I transmit the second annual report of the Commissioner of the Department of Agriculture, asking your attention to the developments in that vital interest of the nation. When Congress assembled a year ago, the war had already lasted nearly twenty months, and there had been many conflicts on both land and sea, with varying results; the rebellion had been pressed back into reduced limits; yet the tone of public feeling and opinion, at home and abroad was not satisfactory. With other signs, the popular elections then just past indicated uneasiness among ourselves, while, amid much that was cold and menacing, the kindest words coming from Europe were uttered in accents of pity that we were too blind to surrender a hopeless cause. Our commerce was suffering greatly by a few armed vessels built upon and furnished from foreign shores, and we were threatened with such additions from the same quarter as would sweep our trade from the sea and raise our blockade. We had failed to elicit from European Governments anything hopeful upon this subject. The preliminary emancipation proclamation, issued in September, was running its assigned period to the beginning of the new year. A month later the final proclamation came, including the announcement that colored men of suitable condition would be received into the war service. The policy of emancipation and of employing black soldiers gave to the future a new aspect, about which hope and fear and doubt contended in uncertain conflict. According to our political system, as a matter of civil administration, the General Government had no lawful power to effect emancipation in any State, and for a long time it had been hoped that the rebellion could be suppressed without resorting to it as a military measure. It was all the while deemed possible that the necessity for it might come, and that if it should the crisis of the contest would then be presented. It came, and, as was anticipated, it was followed by dark and doubtful days. Eleven months having now passed, we are permitted to take another review. The rebel borders are pressed still farther back, and by the complete opening of the Mississippi the country dominated by the rebellion is divided into distinct parts, with no practical communication between them. Tennessee and Arkansas have been substantially cleared of insurgent control, and influential citizens in each, owners of slaves and advocates of slavery at the beginning of the rebellion, now declare openly for emancipation in their respective States. Of those States not included in the emancipation proclamation, Maryland and Missouri, neither of which three years ago would tolerate any restraint upon the extension of slavery into new Territories, only dispute now as to the best mode of removing it within their own limits.

Of those who were slaves at the beginning of the rebellion full 100,000 are now in the United States military service, about one-half of which number actually bear arms in the ranks, thus giving the double advantage of taking so much labor from the insurgent cause and supplying the places which otherwise must be filled with so many white men. So far as tested, it is difficult to say they are not as good soldiers as any. No servile insurrection or tendency to violence or cruelty has marked the measures of emancipation and arming the blacks. These measures have been much discussed in foreign countries, and, contemporary with such discussion, the tone of public sentiment there is much improved. At home the same measures have been fully discussed, supported, criticised, and denounced, and the annual elections following are highly encouraging to those whose official duty it is to bear the country through this great trial. Thus we have the new reckoning. The crisis which threatened to divide the friends of the Union is past.

Looking now to the present and future, and with reference to a resumption of the national authority within the States wherein that authority has been suspended, I have thought fit to issue a proclamation, a copy of which is herewith transmitted.* On examination of this proclamation it will appear, as is believed, that nothing will be attempted beyond what is amply justified by the Constitution. True, the form of an oath is given, but no man is coerced to take it. The man is only promised a pardon in case he voluntarily takes the oath. The Constitution authorizes the Executive to grant or withhold the pardon at his own absolute discretion, and this includes the power to grant on terms, as is fully established by judicial and other authorities.

It is also proffered that if in any of the States named a State government shall be in the mode prescribed set up, such government shall be recognized and guaranteed by the United States, and that under it the State shall, on the constitutional conditions, be protected against invasion and domestic violence. The constitutional obligation of the United States to guarantee to every State in the Union a republican form of government and to protect the State in the cases stated is explicit and full. But why tender the benefits of this provision only to a State government set up in this particular way ? This section of the Constitution contemplates a case wherein the element within a State favorable to republican government in the Union may be too feeble for an opposite and hostile element external to or even within the State, and such are precisely the cases with which we are now dealing.

An attempt to guarantee and protect a revived State government, constructed in whole or in preponderating part from the very element against whose hostility and violence it is to be protected, is simply absurd. There must be a test by which to separate the opposing elements, so as to build only from the sound; and that test is a sufficiently liberal one which accepts as sound whoever will make a sworn recantation of his former unsoundness.

But if it be proper to require as a test of admission to the political body an oath of allegiance to the Constitution of the United States and to the Union under it, why also to the laws and proclamations in regard to slavery? Those laws and proclamations were enacted and put forth for the purpose of aiding in the suppression of the rebellion. To give them their fullest effect there had to be a pledge for their maintenance. In my judgment, they have aided and will further aid the cause for which they were intended. To now abandon them would be not only to relinquish a lever of power, but would also be a cruel and an astounding breach of faith. I may add at this point that while I remain in my present position I shall not attempt to retract or modify the emancipation proclamation, nor shall I return to slavery any person who is free by the terms of that proclamation or by any of the acts of Congress. For these and other reasons it is thought best that support of these measures shall be included in the oath, and it is believed the Executive may lawfully claim it in return for pardon and restoration of forfeited rights, which he has clear constitutional power to withhold altogether or grant upon the terms which he shall deem wisest for the public interest. It should be observed also that this part of the oath is subject to the modifying and abrogating power of legislation and supreme judicial decision.

The proposed acquiescence of the National Executive in any reasonable temporary State arrangement for the freed people is made with the view of possibly modifying the confusion and destitution which must at best attend all classes by a total revolution of labor throughout whole States. It is hoped that the already deeply afflicted people in those States may be somewhat more ready to give up the cause of their affliction if to this extent this vital matter be left to themselves, while no power of the National Executive to prevent an abuse is abridged by the proposition.

The suggestion in the proclamation as to maintaining the political framework of the States on what is called reconstruction is made in the hope that it may do good without danger of harm. It will save labor and avoid great confusion.

But why any proclamation now upon this subject? This question is beset with the conflicting views that the step might be delayed too long or be taken too soon. In some States the elements for resumption seem ready for action. but remain inactive apparently for want of a rallying point—a plan of action. Why shall A adopt the plan of B rather than B that of A? And if A and B should agree, how can they know but that the General Government here will reject their plan? By the proclamation a plan is presented which may be accepted by them as a rallying point, and which they are assured in advance will not be rejected here. This may bring them to act sooner than they otherwise would. The objections to a premature presentation of a plan by the National Executive consist in the danger of committals on points which could be more safely left to further developments. Care has been taken to so shape the document as to avoid embarrassments from this source. Saying that on certain terms certain classes will be pardoned with rights restored, it is not said that other classes or other terms will never be in included. Saying specified way, it is said that reconstruction will be accepted if presented in a not said it will never be accepted in any other way.

The movements by State action for emancipation in several of the States not included in the emancipation proclamation are matters of profound gratulation. And while I do not repeat in detail what I have heretofore so earnestly urged upon this subject, my general views and feelings remain unchanged; and I trust that Congress will omit no fair opportunity of aiding these important steps to a great consummation. In the midst of other cares, however important, we must not lose sight of the fact that the war power is still our main reliance. To that power alone can we look yet for a time to give confidence to the people in the contested regions that the insurgent power will not again overrun them. Until that confidence shall be established little can be done anywhere for what is called reconstruction. Hence our chiefest care must still be directed to the Army and Navy, who have thus far borne their harder part so nobly and well; and it may be esteemed fortunate that in giving the greatest efficiency to these indispensable arms we do also honorably recognize the gallant men, from commander to sentinel, who compose them, and to whom more than to others the world must stand indebted for the home of freedom disenthralled, regenerated, enlarged, and perpetuated.

UNITED STATES DECLARATION OF INDEPENDENCE (1776) BY THE UNITED STATES OF AMERICA IN CONGRESS ASSEMBLED

The United States Declaration of Independence is a statement adopted by the Second Continental Congress on July 4, 1776, announcing that the Thirteen Colonies then at war with Great Britain were no longer a part of the British Empire. Written primarily by Thomas Jefferson, the Declaration is a formal explanation of why Congress had voted on July 2 to declare independence from Great Britain, more than a year after the outbreak of the American Revolutionary War. The birthday of the United States of America—Independence Day—is celebrated on July 4, the day the wording of the Declaration was adopted by the Congress.

Congress issued the Declaration in several forms. The first published version was a typeset broadside printed by John Dunlap, which only listed the names of John Hancock and Charles Thomson as signers. In 1777, Congress issued the Goddard Broadside, which listed all of the signers. What became the most famous version of the Declaration was a handwritten copy signed by the delegates, known as the engrossed version, which is on display in the National Archives in Washington, D.C.

The Declaration of Independence is the first of the three Charters of Freedom along with the Constitution and the Bill of Rights.

In CONGRESS, July 4, 1776.

A DECLARATION

By the REPRESENTATIVES of the

UNITED STATES OF AMERICA,

In GENERAL CONGRESS assembled.

WHEN in the course of human Events, it becomes necessary for one People to dissolve the Political Bands which have connected them with another, and to assume among the Powers of the Earth, the separate and equal Station to which the Laws of Nature and of Nature's God entitle them, a decent Respect to the Opinions of Mankind requires that they should declare the causes which impel them to the Separation.

We hold these Truths to be self-evident, that all Men are created equal, that they are endowed by their Creator with certain unalienable Rights, that among these are Life, Liberty, and the pursuit of Happiness—-That to secure these Rights, Governments are instituted among Men, deriving their just Powers from the Consent of the Governed, that whenever any Form of Government becomes destructive of these Ends, it is the Right of the People to alter or abolish it, and to institute a new Government, laying its Foundation on such Principles, and organizing its Powers in such Form, as to them shall seem most likely to effect their Safety and Happiness. Prudence, indeed, will dictate that Governments long established should not be changed for light and transient Causes; and accordingly all Experience hath shewn, that Mankind are more disposed to suffer, while Evils are sufferable, than to right themselves by abolishing the Forms to which they are accustomed. But when a long Train of Abuses and Usurpations, pursuing invariably the same Object, evinces a Design to reduce them under absolute Despotism, it is their Right, it is their Duty, to throw off such Government, and to provide new Guards for their future Security. Such has been the patient Sufferance of these Colonies; and such is now the Necessity which constrains them to alter their former Systems of Government. The History of the Present King of Great-Britain is a History of repeated Injuries and Usurpations, all having in direct Object the Establishment of an absolute Tyranny over these States. To prove this, let Facts be submitted to a candid World.

He has refused his Assent to Laws, the most wholesome and necessary for the public Good.

He has forbidden his Governors to pass Laws of immediate and pressing Importance, unless suspended in their Operation till his Assent should be obtained; and when so suspended, he has utterly neglected to attend to them.

He has refused to pass other Laws for the Accommodation of large Districts of People; unless those People would relinquish the Right of Representation in the Legislature, a Right inestimable to them, and formidable to Tyrants only.

He has called together Legislative Bodies at Places unusual, uncomfortable, and distant from the Depository of their public Records, for the sole Purpose of fatiguing them into Compliance with his Measures.

He has dissolved Representative Houses repeatedly, for opposing with manly Firmness his Invasions on the Rights of the People.

He has refused for a long Time, after such Dissolutions, to cause others to be elected; whereby the Legislative Powers, incapable of Annihilation, have returned to the People at large for their exercise; the State remaining in the mean time exposed to all the Dangers of Invasion from without, and Convulsions within.

He has endeavoured to prevent the Population of these States; for that Purpose obstructing the Laws for Naturalization of Foreigners; refusing to pass others to encourage their Migrations hither, and raising the Conditions of new Appropriations of Lands.

He has obstructed the Administration of Justice, by refusing his Assent to Laws for establishing Judiciary Powers.

He has made Judges dependent on his Will alone, for the Tenure of their Offices, and the Amount and Payment of their Salaries.

He has erected a Multitude of new Offices, and sent hither Swarms of Officers to harass our People, and eat out their Substance.

He has kept among us, in Times of Peace, Standing Armies, without the consent of our Legislatures.

He has affected to render the Military independent of and superior to the Civil Power.

He has combined with others to subject us to a Jurisdiction foreign to our Constitution, and unacknowledged by our Laws; giving his Assent to their Acts of pretended Legislation:

For quartering large Bodies of Armed Troops among us:

For protecting them, by a mock Trial, from Punishment for any Murders which they should commit on the Inhabitants of these States:

For cutting off our Trade with all Parts of the World:

For imposing taxes on us without our Consent:

For depriving us, in many Cases, of the Benefits of Trial by Jury:

For transporting us beyond Seas to be tried for pretended Offences:

For abolishing the free System of English Laws in a neighbouring Province, establishing therein an arbitrary Government, and enlarging its Boundaries, so as to render it at once an Example and fit Instrument for introducing the same absolute Rule in these Colonies:

For taking away our Charters, abolishing our most valuable Laws, and altering fundamentally the Forms of our Governments:

For suspending our own Legislatures, and declaring themselves invested with Power to legislate for us in all Cases whatsoever:

He has abdicated Government here, by declaring us out of his Protection and waging War against us.

He has plundered our Seas, ravaged our Coasts, burnt our Towns, and destroyed the Lives of our People.

He is, at this Time, transporting large Armies of foreign Mercenaries to compleat the Works of Death, Desolation, and Tyranny, already begun with circumstances of Cruelty and Perfidy, scarcely paralleled in the most barbarous Ages, and totally unworthy the Head of a civilized Nation.

He has constrained our fellow Citizens taken Captive on the high Seas to bear Arms against their Country, to become the Executioners of their Friends and Brethren, or to fall themselves by their Hands.

He has excited domestic Insurrections amongst us, and has endeavoured to bring on the Inhabitants of our Frontiers, the merciless Indian Savages, whose known Rule of Warfare, is an undistinguished Destruction, of all Ages, Sexes and Conditions.

In every stage of these Oppressions we have Petitioned for Redress in the most humble Terms: Our repeated Petitions have been answered only by repeated Injury. A Prince, whose Character is thus marked by every act which may define a Tyrant, is unfit to be the Ruler of a free People.

Nor have we been wanting in Attentions to our British Brethren. We have warned them from Time to Time of Attempts by their Legislature to extend an unwarrantable Jurisdiction over us. We have reminded them of the Circumstances of our Emigration and Settlement here. We have appealed to their native Justice and Magnanimity, and we have conjured them by the Ties of common Kindred to disavow these Usurpations, which, would inevitably interrupt our Connections and Correspondence. They too have been deaf to the Voice of Justice and of Consanguinity. We must, therefore, acquiesce in the Necessity, which denounces our Separation, and hold them, as we hold the rest of Mankind, Enemies in War, in Peace, Friends.

We, therefore, the Representatives of the UNITED STATES OF AMERICA, in General Congress, Assembled, appealing to the Supreme Judge of the World for the Rectitude of our Intentions, do, in the Name, and by Authority of the good People of these Colonies, solemnly Publish and Declare, That these United Colonies are, and of Right ought to be, Free and Independent States; that they are absolved from all Allegiance to the British Crown, and that all political Connection between them and the State of Great-Britain, is and ought to be totally dissolved; and that as Free and Independent States, they have full Power to levy War, conclude Peace, contract Alliances, establish Commerce, and to do all other Acts and Things which

Independent States may of right do. And for the support of this Declaration, with a firm Reliance on the Protection of the divine Providence, we mutually pledge to each other our Lives, our Fortunes, and our sacred Honor.

Signed by Order and in Behalf of the Congress,

JOHN HANCOCK, President.

CONSTITUTION OF THE UNITED STATES OF AMERICA (1787) BY THE FEDERAL CONVENTION OF 1787

The Constitution of the United States of America is the supreme law of the United States of America. It was completed on September 17, 1787, with its adoption by the Constitutional Convention in Philadelphia, Pennsylvania, and was later ratified by special conventions in each state. It created a federal union of sovereign states, and a federal government to operate that union. It replaced the less defined union that had existed under the Articles of Confederation. It took effect on March 4, 1789 and has served as a model for the constitutions of numerous other nations. The Constitution of the United States of America is the oldest written national constitution in use.

We the People of the United States, in Order to form a more perfect Union, establish Justice, insure domestic Tranquility, provide for the common defence, promote the general Welfare, and secure the Blessings of Liberty to ourselves and our Posterity, do ordain and establish this Constitution for the United States of America.

Article. I.

Section. 1.

All legislative Powers herein granted shall be vested in a Congress of the United States, which shall consist of a Senate and House of Representatives.

Section. 2.

The House of Representatives shall be composed of Members chosen every second Year by the People of the several States, and the Electors in each State shall have the Qualifications requisite for Electors of the most numerous Branch of the State Legislature.

No Person shall be a Representative who shall not have attained to the age of twenty five Years, and been seven Years a Citizen of the United States, and who shall not, when elected, be an Inhabitant of that State in which he shall be chosen.

Representatives and direct Taxes shall be apportioned among the several States which may be included within this Union, according to their respective Numbers, which shall be determined by adding to the whole Number of free Persons, including those bound to Service for a Term of Years, and excluding Indians not taxed, three fifths of all other Persons. The actual Enumeration shall be made within three Years after the first Meeting of the Congress of the United States, and within every subsequent Term of ten Years, in such Manner as they shall by Law direct. The Number of Representatives shall not exceed one for every thirty Thousand, but each State shall have at Least one Representative; and until such enumeration shall be made, the State of New Hampshire shall be entitled to chuse three, Massachusetts eight, Rhode-Island and Providence Plantations one, Connecticut five, New-York six, New Jersey four, Pennsylvania eight, Delaware one, Maryland six, Virginia ten, North Carolina five, South Carolina five, and Georgia three.

When vacancies happen in the Representation from any State, the Executive Authority thereof shall issue Writs of Election to fill such Vacancies.

The House of Representatives shall chuse their Speaker and other Officers; and shall have the sole Power of Impeachment.

Section. 3.

The Senate of the United States shall be composed of two Senators from each State, chosen by the Legislature thereof, for six Years; and each Senator shall have one Vote.

Immediately after they shall be assembled in Consequence of the first Election, they shall be divided as equally as may be into three Classes. The Seats of the Senators of the first Class shall be vacated at the Expiration of the second Year, of the second Class at the Expiration of the fourth Year, and of the third Class at the Expiration of the sixth Year, so that one third may be chosen every second Year; and if Vacancies happen by Resignation, or otherwise, during the Recess of the Legislature of any State, the Executive thereof may make temporary Appointments until the next Meeting of the Legislature, which shall then fill such Vacancies.

No Person shall be a Senator who shall not have attained to the Age of thirty Years, and been nine Years a Citizen of the United States, and who shall not, when elected, be an Inhabitant of that State for which he shall be chosen.

The Vice President of the United States shall be President of the Senate but shall have no Vote, unless they be equally divided.

The Senate shall chuse their other Officers, and also a President pro tempore, in the Absence of the Vice President, or when he shall exercise the Office of President of the United States.

The Senate shall have the sole Power to try all Impeachments. When sitting for that Purpose, they shall be on Oath or Affirmation. When the President of the United States is tried the Chief Justice shall preside: And no Person shall be convicted without the Concurrence of two thirds of the Members present.

Judgment in Cases of Impeachment shall not extend further than to removal from Office, and disqualification to hold and enjoy any Office of honor, Trust or Profit under the United States: but the Party convicted shall nevertheless be liable and subject to Indictment, Trial, Judgment and Punishment, according to Law.

Section. 4.

The Times, Places and Manner of holding Elections for Senators and Representatives, shall be prescribed in each State by the Legislature thereof; but the Congress may at any time by Law make or alter such Regulations, except as to the Places of chusing Senators.

The Congress shall assemble at least once in every Year, and such Meeting shall be on the first Monday in December, unless they shall by Law appoint a different Day.

Section. 5.

Each House shall be the Judge of the Elections, Returns and Qualifications of its own Members, and a Majority of each shall constitute a Quorum to do Business; but a smaller Number may adjourn from day to day, and may be authorized to compel the Attendance of absent Members, in such Manner, and under such Penalties as each House may provide.

Each House may determine the Rules of its Proceedings, punish its Members for disorderly Behaviour, and, with the Concurrence of two thirds, expel a Member.

Each House shall keep a Journal of its Proceedings, and from time to time publish the same, excepting such Parts as may in their Judgment require Secrecy; and the Yeas and Nays of the Members of either House on any question shall, at the Desire of one fifth of those Present, be entered on the Journal.

Neither House, during the Session of Congress, shall, without the Consent of the other, adjourn for more than three days, nor to any other Place than that in which the two Houses shall be sitting.

Section. 6.

The Senators and Representatives shall receive a Compensation for their Services, to be ascertained by Law, and paid out of the Treasury of the United States. They shall in all Cases, except Treason, Felony and Breach of the Peace, be privileged from Arrest during their Attendance at the Session of their respective Houses, and in going to and returning from the same; and for any Speech or Debate in either House, they shall not be questioned in any other Place.

No Senator or Representative shall, during the Time for which he was elected, be appointed to any civil Office under the Authority of the United States, which shall have been created, or the Emoluments whereof shall have been encreased during such time; and no Person holding any Office under the United States, shall be a Member of either House during his Continuance in Office.

Section. 7.

All Bills for raising Revenue shall originate in the House of Representatives; but the Senate may propose or concur with amendments as on other Bills.

Every Bill which shall have passed the House of Representatives and the Senate, shall, before it become a law, be presented to the President of the United States: If he approve he shall sign it, but if not he shall return it, with his Objections to that House in which it shall have originated, who shall enter the Objections at large on their Journal, and proceed to reconsider it. If after such Reconsideration two thirds of that House shall agree to pass the Bill, it shall be sent, together with the Objections, to the other House, by which it shall likewise be reconsidered, and if approved by two thirds of that House, it shall become a Law. But in all such Cases the Votes of both Houses shall be determined by Yeas and Nays, and the Names of the Persons voting for and against the Bill shall be entered on the Journal of each House respectively. If any Bill shall not be returned by the President within ten Days (Sundays excepted) after it shall have been presented to him, the Same shall be a Law, in like Manner as if he had signed it, unless the Congress by their Adjournment prevent its Return, in which Case it shall not be a Law.

Every Order, Resolution, or Vote to which the Concurrence of the Senate and House of Representatives may be necessary (except on a question of Adjournment) shall be presented to the President of the United States; and before the Same shall take Effect, shall be approved by him, or being disapproved by him, shall be repassed by two thirds of the Senate and House of Representatives, according to the Rules and Limitations prescribed in the Case of a Bill.

Section. 8.

The Congress shall have Power To lay and collect Taxes, Duties, Imposts and Excises, to pay the Debts and provide for the common Defence and general Welfare of the United States; but all Duties, Imposts and Excises shall be uniform throughout the United States;

To borrow Money on the credit of the United States;

To regulate Commerce with foreign Nations, and among the several States, and with the Indian Tribes;

To establish an uniform Rule of Naturalization, and uniform Laws on the subject of Bankruptcies throughout the United States;

To coin Money, regulate the Value thereof, and of foreign Coin, and fix the Standard of Weights and Measures;

To provide for the Punishment of counterfeiting the Securities and current Coin of the United States;

To establish Post Offices and post Roads;

To promote the Progress of Science and useful Arts, by securing for limited Times to Authors and Inventors the exclusive Right to their respective Writings and Discoveries;

To constitute Tribunals inferior to the supreme Court;

To define and punish Piracies and Felonies committed on the high Seas, and Offences against the Law of Nations;

To declare War, grant Letters of Marque and Reprisal, and make Rules concerning Captures on Land and Water;

To raise and support Armies, but no Appropriation of Money to that Use shall be for a longer Term than two Years;

To provide and maintain a Navy;

To make Rules for the Government and Regulation of the land and naval Forces;

To provide for calling forth the Militia to execute the Laws of the Union, suppress Insurrections and repel Invasions;

To provide for organizing, arming, and disciplining, the Militia, and for governing such Part of them as may be employed in the Service of the United States, reserving to the States respectively, the Appointment of the Officers, and the Authority of training the Militia according to the discipline prescribed by Congress;

To exercise exclusive Legislation in all Cases whatsoever, over such District (not exceeding ten Miles square) as may, by Cession of Particular States, and the Acceptance of Congress, become the Seat of the Government of the United States, and to exercise like Authority over all Places purchased by the Consent of the Legislature of the State in which the Same shall be, for the Erection of Forts, Magazines, Arsenals, dock-Yards and other needful Buildings;—And

To make all Laws which shall be necessary and proper for carrying into Execution the foregoing Powers and all other Powers vested by this Constitution in the Government of the United States, or in any Department or Officer thereof.

Section. 9.

The Migration or Importation of such Persons as any of the States now existing shall think proper to admit, shall not be prohibited by the Congress prior to the Year one thousand eight hundred and eight, but a Tax or duty may be imposed on such Importation, not exceeding ten dollars for each Person.

The Privilege of the Writ of Habeas Corpus shall not be suspended, unless when in Cases of Rebellion or Invasion the public Safety may require it.

No Bill of Attainder or ex post facto Law shall be passed.

No Capitation, or other direct, Tax shall be laid, unless in Proportion to the Census or Enumeration herein before directed to be taken.

No Tax or Duty shall be laid on Articles exported from any State.

No Preference shall be given by any Regulation of Commerce or Revenue to the Ports of one State over those of another: nor shall Vessels bound to, or from, one State, be obliged to enter, clear or pay Duties in another.

No Money shall be drawn from the Treasury, but in Consequence of Appropriations made by Law; and a regular Statement and Account of the Receipts and Expenditures of all public Money shall be published from time to time.

No Title of Nobility shall be granted by the United States: And no Person holding any Office of Profit or Trust under them, shall, without the Consent of the Congress, accept of any present, Emolument, Office, or Title, of any kind whatever, from any King, Prince or foreign State.

Section. 10.

No State shall enter into any Treaty, Alliance, or Confederation; grant Letters of Marque and Reprisal; coin Money; emit Bills of Credit; make any Thing but gold and silver Coin a Tender in Payment of Debts; pass any Bill of Attainder, ex post facto Law, or Law impairing the Obligation of Contracts, or grant any Title of Nobility.

No State shall, without the Consent of the Congress, lay any Imposts or Duties on Imports or Exports, except what may be absolutely necessary for executing it's inspection Laws: and the net Produce of all Duties and Imposts, laid by any State on Imports or Exports, shall be for the Use of the Treasury of the United States; and all such Laws shall be subject to the Revision and Controul of the Congress.

No State shall, without the Consent of Congress, lay any Duty of Tonnage, keep Troops, or Ships of War in time of Peace, enter into any Agreement or Compact with another State, or with a foreign Power, or engage in War, unless actually invaded, or in such imminent Danger as will not admit of delay.

Article. II.

Section. 1.

The executive Power shall be vested in a President of the United States of America. He shall hold his Office during the Term of four Years, and, together with the Vice President, chosen for the same Term, be elected, as follows:

Each State shall appoint, in such Manner as the Legislature thereof may direct, a Number of Electors, equal to the whole Number of Senators and Representatives to which the State may be entitled in the Congress: but no Senator or Representative, or Person holding an Office of Trust or Profit under the United States, shall be appointed an Elector.

The Electors shall meet in their respective States, and vote by Ballot for two Persons, of whom one at least shall not be an Inhabitant of the same State with themselves. And they shall make a List of all the Persons voted for, and of the Number of Votes for each; which List they shall sign and certify, and transmit sealed to the Seat of the Government of the United States, directed to the President of the Senate. The President of the Senate shall, in the Presence of the Senate and House of Representatives, open all the Certificates, and the Votes shall then be counted. The Person having the greatest Number of Votes shall be the President, if such Number be a Majority of the whole Number of Electors appointed; and if there be more than one who have such Majority, and have an equal Number of Votes, then the House of Representatives shall immediately chuse by Ballot one of them for President; and if no Person have a Majority, then from the five highest on the List the said House shall in like Manner chuse the President. But in chusing the President, the Votes shall be taken by States, the Representation from each State having one Vote; a quorum for this Purpose shall consist of a Member or Members from two thirds of the States, and a Majority of all the States shall be necessary to a Choice. In every Case, after the Choice of the President, the Person having the greatest Number of Votes of the Electors shall be the Vice President. But if there should remain two or more who have equal Votes, the Senate shall chuse from them by Ballot the Vice President.

The Congress may determine the Time of chusing the Electors, and the Day on which they shall give their Votes; which Day shall be the same throughout the United States.

No Person except a natural born Citizen, or a Citizen of the United States, at the time of the Adoption of this Constitution, shall be eligible to the Office of President; neither shall any person be eligible to that Office who shall not have attained to the Age of thirty five Years, and been fourteen Years a Resident within the United States.

In Case of the Removal of the President from Office, or of his Death, Resignation, or Inability to discharge the Powers and Duties of the said Office, the Same shall devolve on the Vice President, and the Congress may by Law provide for the Case of Removal, Death, Resignation or Inability, both of the President and Vice President, declaring what Officer shall then act as President, and such Officer shall act accordingly, until the Disability be removed, or a President shall be elected.

The President shall, at stated Times, receive for his Services, a Compensation, which shall neither be encreased nor diminished during the Period for which he shall have been elected, and he shall not receive within that Period any other Emolument from the United States, or any of them.

Before he enter on the Execution of his Office, he shall take the following Oath or Affirmation:—"I do solemnly swear (or affirm) that I will faithfully execute the Office of President of the United States, and will to the best of my Ability, preserve, protect and defend the Constitution of the United States."

Section. 2.

The President shall be Commander in Chief of the Army and Navy of the United States, and of the Militia of the several States, when called into the actual Service of the United States; he may require the Opinion, in writing, of the principal Officer in each of the executive Departments, upon any Subject relating to the Duties of their respective Offices, and he shall have Power to Grant Reprieves and Pardons for Offences against the United States, except in Cases of Impeachment.

He shall have Power, by and with the Advice and Consent of the Senate, to make Treaties, provided two thirds of the Senators present concur; and he shall nominate, and by and with the Advice and Consent of the Senate, shall appoint Ambassadors, other public Ministers and Consuls, Judges of the supreme Court, and all other Officers of the United States, whose Appointments are not herein otherwise provided for, and which shall be established by Law: but the Congress may by Law vest the Appointment of such inferior Officers, as they think proper, in the President alone, in the Courts of Law, or in the Heads of Departments.

The President shall have Power to fill up all Vacancies that may happen during the Recess of the Senate, by granting Commissions which shall expire at the End of their next Session.

Section. 3.

He shall from time to time give to the Congress Information of the State of the Union, and recommend to their Consideration such Measures as he shall judge necessary and expedient; he may, on extraordinary Occasions, convene both Houses, or either of them, and in Case of Disagreement between them, with Respect to the Time of Adjournment, he may adjourn them to such Time as he shall think proper; he shall receive Ambassadors and other public Ministers; he shall take Care that the Laws be faithfully executed, and shall Commission all the Officers of the United States.

Section. 4.

The President, Vice President and all Civil Officers of the United States, shall be removed from Office on Impeachment for and Conviction of, Treason, Bribery, or other high Crimes and Misdemeanors.

Article. III.

Section. 1.

The judicial Power of the United States, shall be vested in one supreme Court, and in such inferior Courts as the Congress may from time to time ordain and establish. The Judges, both of the supreme and inferior Courts, shall hold their Offices during good Behaviour, and shall, at stated Times, receive for their Services, a Compensation, which shall not be diminished during their Continuance in Office.

Section. 2.

The judicial Power shall extend to all Cases, in Law and Equity, arising under this Constitution, the Laws of the United States, and Treaties made, or which shall be made, under their Authority;—to all Cases affecting Ambassadors, other public ministers and Consuls;— to all Cases of admiralty and maritime Jurisdiction;—to Controversies to which the United States shall be a Party;—to Controversies between two or more States;—between a State and Citizens of another State;—between Citizens of different States;—between Citizens of the same State claiming Lands under Grants of different States, and between a State, or the Citizens thereof, and foreign States, Citizens or Subjects.

In all Cases affecting Ambassadors, other public Ministers and Consuls, and those in which a State shall be Party, the supreme Court shall have original Jurisdiction. In all the other Cases before mentioned, the supreme Court shall have appellate Jurisdiction, both as to Law and Fact, with such Exceptions, and under such Regulations as the Congress shall make.

The Trial of all Crimes, except in Cases of Impeachment, shall be by Jury; and such Trial shall be held in the State where the said Crimes shall have been committed; but when not committed within any State, the Trial shall be at such Place or Places as the Congress may by Law have directed.

Section. 3.

Treason against the United States, shall consist only in levying War against them, or in adhering to their Enemies, giving them Aid and Comfort. No Person shall be convicted of Treason unless on the Testimony of two Witnesses to the same overt Act, or on Confession in open Court.

The Congress shall have Power to declare the Punishment of Treason, but no Attainder of Treason shall work Corruption of Blood, or Forfeiture except during the Life of the Person attainted.

Article. IV.

Section. 1.

Full Faith and Credit shall be given in each State to the public Acts, Records, and judicial Proceedings of every other State. And the Congress may by general Laws prescribe the Manner in which such Acts, Records and Proceedings shall be proved, and the Effect thereof.

Section. 2.

The Citizens of each State shall be entitled to all Privileges and Immunities of Citizens in the several States.

A Person charged in any State with Treason, Felony, or other Crime, who shall flee from Justice, and be found in another State, shall on Demand of the executive Authority of the State from which he fled, be delivered up, to be removed to the State having Jurisdiction of the Crime.

No Person held to Service or Labour in one State, under the Laws thereof, escaping into another, shall, in Consequence of any Law or Regulation therein, be discharged from such Service or Labour, but shall be delivered up on Claim of the Party to whom such Service or Labour may be due.

Section. 3.

New States may be admitted by the Congress into this Union; but no new State shall be formed or erected within the Jurisdiction of any other State; nor any State be formed by the Junction of two or more States, or Parts of States, without the Consent of the Legislatures of the States concerned as well as of the Congress.

The Congress shall have Power to dispose of and make all needful Rules and Regulations respecting the Territory or other Property belonging to the United States; and nothing in this Constitution shall be so construed as to Prejudice any Claims of the United States, or of any particular State.

Section. 4.

The United States shall guarantee to every State in this Union a Republican Form of Government, and shall protect each of them against Invasion; and on Application of the Legislature, or of the Executive (when the Legislature cannot be convened) against domestic Violence.

Article. V.

The Congress, whenever two thirds of both Houses shall deem it necessary, shall propose Amendments to this Constitution, or, on the Application of the Legislatures of two thirds of the several States, shall call a Convention for proposing Amendments, which, in either Case, shall be valid to all Intents and Purposes, as Part of this Constitution, when ratified by the Legislatures of three fourths of the several States, or by Conventions in three fourths thereof, as the one or the other Mode of Ratification may be proposed by the Congress; Provided that no Amendment which may be made prior to the Year One thousand eight hundred and eight shall in any Manner affect the first and fourth Clauses in the Ninth Section of the first Article; and that no State, without its Consent, shall be deprived of its equal Suffrage in the Senate.

Article. VI.

All Debts contracted and Engagements entered into, before the Adoption of this Constitution, shall be as valid against the United States under this Constitution, as under the Confederation.

This Constitution, and the Laws of the United States which shall be made in Pursuance thereof; and all Treaties made, or which shall be made, under the Authority of the United States, shall be the supreme Law of the Land; and the Judges in every State shall be bound thereby, any Thing in the Constitution or Laws of any state to the Contrary notwithstanding.

The Senators and Representatives before mentioned, and the Members of the several State Legislatures, and all executive and judicial Officers, both of the United States and of the several States, shall be bound by Oath or Affirmation, to support this Constitution; but no religious Test shall ever be required as a Qualification to any Office or public Trust under the United States.

Article. VII.

The Ratification of the Conventions of nine States, shall be sufficient for the Establishment of this Constitution between the States so ratifying the same.

BILL OF RIGHTS (1791) UNITED STATES CONGRESS

In the United States, the Bill of Rights is the term for the first ten amendments to the United States Constitution. These amendments explicitly limit the Federal government's powers, protecting the rights of the people by preventing Congress from abridging freedom of speech, freedom of the press, freedom of assembly, freedom of religious worship, and the right to bear arms, preventing unreasonable search and seizure, cruel and unusual punishment, and self-incrimination, and guaranteeing due process of law and a speedy public trial with an impartial jury. In addition, the Bill of Rights states that "the enumeration in the Constitution, of certain rights, shall not be construed to deny or disparage others retained by the people," and reserves all powers not specifically granted to the Federal government to the citizenry or States. These amendments came into effect on December 15, 1791, when ratified by three-fourths of the States.

Congress OF THE United States, begun and held at the City of New-York, on Wednesday the fourth of March, one thousand seven hundred and eighty nine.

THE Conventions of a number of the States, having at the time of their adopting the Constitution, expressed a desire, in order to prevent misconstruction or abuse of its powers, that further declaratory and restrictive clauses should be added; And as extending the ground of public confidence in the Government, will best ensure the beneficent ends of its institution.

RESOLVED by the Senate and House of Representatives of the United States of America, in Congress assembled, two thirds of both Houses concurring, that the following Articles be proposed to the Legislatures of the several States, as amendments to the Constitution of the United States, all, or any of which Articles, when ratified by three-fourths of the said Legislatures, to be valid to all intents and purposes, as part of the said Constitution; viz.

ARTICLES in addition to, and Amendment of the Constitution of the United States of America, proposed by Congress, and ratified by the Legislatures of the several States, pursuant to the fifth Article of the original Constitution.

Article the first. .... After the first enumeration required by the first article of the Constitution, there shall be one Representative for every 30,000 until the number shall amount to 100, after which the proportion shall be so regulated by Congress, that there shall be not less than 100 Representatives, nor less than one Representative for every 40,000 persons, until the number of Representatives shall amount to 200; after which the proportion shall be so regulated by Congress, that there shall not be less than 200 Representatives, nor more than one Representative for every 50,000 persons.

Article the second ... No law, varying the compensation for the services of the Senators and Representatives, shall take effect, until an election of Representatives shall have intervened.

Article the third...... Congress shall make no law respecting an establishment of religion, or prohibiting the free exercise thereof; or abridging the freedom of speech, or of the press; or the right of the people peaceably to assemble, and to petition the Government for a redress of grievances.

Article the fourth..... A well regulated Militia, being necessary to the security of a free state, the right of the people to keep and bear arms, shall not be infringed.

Article the fifth....... No soldier shall, in time of peace be quartered in any house, without the consent of the owner, nor in time of war, but in a manner to be prescribed by law.

Article the sixth...... The right of the people to be secure in their persons, houses, papers, and effects, against unreasonable searches and seizures, shall not be violated, and no Warrants shall issue, but upon probable cause, supported by Oath or affirmation, and particularly describing the place to be searched, and the persons or things to be seized.

Article the seventh... No person shall be held to answer for a capital, or otherwise infamous crime, unless on a presentment or indictment of a Grand Jury, except in cases arising in the land or naval forces, or in the Militia, when in actual service in time of war or public danger; nor shall any person be subject for the same offence to be twice put in jeopardy of life or limb; nor shall be compelled in any criminal case to be a witness against himself, nor be deprived of life, liberty, or property, without due process of law; nor shall private property be taken for public use, without just compensation.

Article the eighth... In all criminal prosecutions, the accused shall enjoy the right to a speedy and public trial, by an impartial jury of the State and district wherein the crime shall have been committed, which district shall have been previously ascertained by law, and to be informed of the nature and cause of the accusation; to be confronted with the witnesses against him; to have compulsory process for obtaining witnesses in his favor, and to have the Assistance of Counsel for his defense.

Article the ninth... In suits at common law, where the value in controversy shall exceed twenty dollars, the right of trial by jury shall be preserved, and no fact tried by a jury, shall be otherwise re-examined in any Court of the United States, than according to the rules of the common law.

Article the tenth.... Excessive bail shall not be required, nor excessive fines imposed, nor cruel and unusual punishments inflicted.

Article the eleventh.... The enumeration in the Constitution, of certain rights, shall not be construed to deny or disparage others retained by the people.

Article the twelfth ... The powers not delegated to the United States by the Constitution, nor prohibited by it to the States, are reserved to the States respectively, or to the people."

Manufactured by Amazon.ca
Acheson, AB

13851377R00069